C000294279

THE FISHING
POCKET COMPANION

Lesley Crawford

PAVILION

A Think Book for Pavilion Books

This edition published by Pavilion Books in 2007
First published in the United Kingdom in 2004 by Robson Books
10 Southcombe Street, London W14 0RA

Imprints of Anova Books Company Ltd

Text and design © Think Publishing 2004
The moral rights of the authors have been asserted

Edited by Lesley Crawford
The Companion team: Tilly Boulter, James Collins,
Rhiannon Guy, Emma Jones, Lou Millward Tait, Matt Packer,
Sonja Patel, Jo Swinnerton and Malcolm Tait

Think Publishing
The Pall Mall Deposit
124-128 Barlby Road, London W10 6BL
www.thinkpublishing.co.uk

ISBN 978-1-862057-92-0

2 4 6 8 10 9 7 5 3 1

Printed and bound by Millenium International Printing, China

www.anovabooks.com

THE POCKET COMPANION SERIES:
COLLECT THEM ALL

The Traveller's
Pocket Companion
by Georgina Newbery
and Rhiannon Guy
ISBN 978-1-862057-91-3

The Walker's
Pocket Companion
by Malcolm Tait
ISBN 978-1-862057-93-7

The Cook's
Pocket Companion
by Jo Swinnerton
ISBN 978-1-862057-90-6

INTRODUCTION

Angling has, without a doubt, the largest library of any sport. Since Dame Juliana and her much analysed work of 1496, *The Treatyse of Fyshynge with an Angle*, its good disciples have churned out many thousands of volumes dedicated to this most baffling of pastimes. Of course, much of the work is technical – and some too dull to even mention. But there is another side. Angling, in its time, has bewitched the likes of Shakespeare, Shelley and Keats. Wordsworth was known to walk 10 miles for a decent spot of piking and we all know of Hemingway's obsession with the sport.

But where do you start when faced with such a vast array of penmanship? I must admit that I have a library of well over three thousand angling books, some of which I have even read. Despite this I return most often to just a few titles, all of them either anthologies or little curios; books you can just dip into and pick out the juicy bits. Nothing too taxing. For sheer size and scope there is *Paxman's Fish, Fishing and the Meaning of Life*. On a smaller scale, but probably even better is *The Magic Wheel*, by David Profumo and Graham Swift. But way out front, in my humble opinion, is the magnificent *Angler's Weekend Book* by Eric Taverner and John Moore.

Since 1938 the *Angler's Weekend Book* has reigned supreme as a book full of absolutely wonderful trivia. Until now. With *The Fishing Pocket Companion*, Lesley Crawford has come close to pushing it off its perch. It contains such gems as how to ruin your catch, cockney rhyming slang for fly casters, unrequited love and salmon in a basket. Need I say more?

Jon Ward-Allen Editor, *Waterlog* magazine

UNREQUITED LOVE

In the UK and particularly in Scotland, the unusual and not very endearing term 'baggot' (the equivalent of the male sea trout kelt) is applied to a female sea trout that has been thwarted in love. While all other fish have cheerfully managed to procreate, the poor dear baggot has not been able to spawn and shed her eggs. Baggots are to be found in their natal stream, or in inland freshwater lakes or lochs where they are lingering (probably in a deep sulk) and lying low after the unsuccessful attempt they made at spawning in the previous winter. These fish are sometimes caught by anglers in early spring and, if captured, should be returned live to the water. This is particularly important for continuation of the species, for unlike the male kelt, who often dies after the rigours of spawning, the baggot will usually make a recovery and may go on to reproduce more happily in future seasons.

A BIT FISHY

Anagram
What's on the end of your line?
PELTBRED LIAILY
Answer on page 144.

SEXY FISH

In pre-Christian times the Greek fish goddess, Aphrodite Salacia, was worshipped by her followers on a special designated day, a Friday. On this day they consumed a large helping of fish and then enjoyed an orgy for dessert. From this Greek goddess's first name comes the English month of April, and from her second name comes the English word salacious. The practice of eating fish on Fridays was continued in the Christian world, though the orgy seems to have been dropped, or at least is not so well publicised.

FISH WARS

Pirating Patagonians

Not many of us realise that in the seas of Antarctica, the sea bass is known as the Patagonian toothfish. So valuable has this fish become – 10 dollars a kilo or more is common – it has gained the name 'white gold'. Illegal poaching of these sea bass occurs mainly in the rich waters of the Southern Ocean. Despite these seas being covered by the Convention for Conservation of Antarctic Marine Living Resources (CCAMLR), a grim game of cat and mouse is being played out daily with 'pirate' trawlers setting down illegal nets, hauling in a catch and then swiftly racing away from policing navy vessels. The pirates are sophisticated in their methods, registering their boats under flags of convenience, falsifying log books, obliterating the names of their boats, and using radar to evade conservation patrols. With funding for the trawlers' crews and their equipment thought to come from less than ethical business sources, this is a war that may not end soon.

A STINGING LINE

In Anglo-Saxon days, fishing nets and lines were made out of nettle hemp. The nettles would be gathered in spring or early summer, the leaves removed and the stems would be soaked in water, pulped and then long stringy fibres drawn out and spun together to form a yarn. The process was rather similar to flax or wool spinning, and the resultant hemp was strong and durable. The fishermen would then use their nettle hemp nets to take fish from both sea and river. Whether fish being captured by this ruse ever gave rise to the catch phrase 'caught in a sting' is not known.

CASTING OFF

In the *New English Dictionary*, to cast means to shed, throw, direct, spread or transmit. You might therefore think that the cast, that quintessentially artistic action of propelling line and hook upon the water, has been with us since man first went angling. Truth is, it hasn't. The very first rods used were so long and cumbersome that to cast anything with the line tied at the sharp end was, well, nigh impossible. In the seventeenth century Colonel Venables did mention casting a fly, 'Be sure in casting, that your fly fall first onto the water', but this was more to do with simply extending the pole over the river and letting the wind blow the line and the attached fly about on the water surface. It was not until the mid nineteenth century, when reels to store the line on came into vogue, that actual methods of casting began to be recorded. Ronalds, circa 1836, takes the trouble to describe how to propel the fly to the water in a 'uniform sweep or curve' round the head. This description was probably the first on what we now know as overhead casting. From then on, fly casting advanced through switch, steeple, roll, single and double spey casts to name but a few. Casting gurus, instructors and demonstrators for these styles of casting remain in great demand, especially amongst lesser mortals not quite able to so elegantly waft the wand.

FISHY FIGURES

151

Number of seconds you must not exceed, when landing a virtual sailfish in the Miami Boot Show Annual Billfish Tournament

I'll get to the blighters any way I can...

FUNKY REDDS FISH

American and British attitudes to recreational fishing during spawning time are poles apart. The Brits close their fisheries when fish are in the act of procreation, whereas the Americans carry on angling. In fact American anglers set great store by fishing techniques that can be used at this time. According to a March 2005 report on www.yellowstoneangler.com: 'Some big rainbows have moved into the creeks to spawn. Due to their funky spawning behaviour, spot fishing has become extremely easy and the fish are less selective than normal. An egg pattern, fished behind a redd [a nest-like indentation in the gravel into which the female fish will shed eggs] can be a very effective technique.' The reporter then warns anglers to watch where they are walking, and not to squeeze any eggs out when releasing fish.

It was reported also on the website that there was to be a series of meetings over the fate of the native cutthroat trout, which is in severe decline in the Yellowstone region. Could coitus interruptus have something to do with it?

SCOTLAND'S ALL-BUT-FORGOTTEN TWENTIETH-CENTURY FISHING HEROES

V Carron Wellington

V Carron Wellington wrote only one book, which was published in 1952 and was entitled *The Adventures of a Sporting Angler*. In it he records, with huge verbosity but little pomposity, his escapades while fishing in the remoter areas of Scotland. Wellington was an eccentric angler in the Harrison Ford mould; in fact *Raiders of the Lost Ark* could have been modelled on him, except that it would have been called 'Raiders of the Lost Loch'. He is best known for stripping off, clenching his fishing rod between his teeth and swimming out to inaccessible islands on lochs when no boat was available. Despite Wellington's modern-day obscurity, anglers who accidentally pick up a copy of his long-winded book in some dusty corner of an old bookshop might suddenly find they feel compelled to seek out trout in wild remote places, following in the footsteps of Wellington's boots.

FISH FACTS

1. Fish are intellectual beings capable of higher thought and reasoning.
2. Fish see you coming.
3. Fish show steely determination in ignoring your fly or bait.
4. Fish attach themselves to other anglers' lines out of spite.
5. Fish put their heads up only when they see you packing up and/or leaving.
6. Fish know when you have a stinking hangover from the night before.
7. Fish know when you don't know much about them.
8. Fish go on holiday the same time as you do.

BRITAIN'S FISHING FASHIONS

Welsh night birds

It's a well-known fact that when the Welsh sewin (sea trout) are in the rivers, Welsh anglers only come out at night. This is because to fish during the day is angling suicide; the gin-clear rivers of Wales mean these wary fish see you way before you see them. Even walking along the bank in daytime will result in the fish departing in droves, and that's before you've put the rod up. To cope with this need for nocturnal angling the Welsh adopt certain strategies. To follow in their footsteps, you need to enhance your night vision (a few carrots might help); then you need to develop the knack of surviving on two hours of sleep; and, finally, you must develop a commando mentality of familiarising yourself with every stone, ditch and ledge on the river in daylight so when you fish in darkness, you avoid upending yourself straight into some very cold water.

I'LL BE BACK

It seems there is a distinctly chilly air between fishermen and administrators when it comes to deciding the future care of Californian coastal waters. On the one hand Governor Schwarzenegger has directed his local authorities to establish a string of marine reserves or fish conservation areas along the State's coastline. Such Marine Protected Areas (MPAs) are supposed to be oceanic refuges where all aquatic species can live free from fishing pressure. However, dismayed big game fishermen are now calling such measures draconian, as the sites of the reserves are near the shoreline where the fish stocks are at their healthiest. Anglers also feel that such sweeping 'no fishing' policies advertised on local TV networks are inflammatory and, not surprisingly, a war of words has ensued. Could it be that the illustrious Governor is simply not a fishing fan?

11

WALLEYE NEVER

In January 2005, the Rev Mariusz Zajac caught a record walleye (pollack) while ice fishing in his local lake in remote Saskatchewan. At 18.3 pounds this was a new world record for ice-caught walleye and he quickly posted his success on the internet. Unfortunately a prankster then relayed a picture of the Reverend posing with his catch to many different websites, changing the location of the catch each time he sent the picture out. The fish appeared not only to have been caught in Saskatchewan but also Manitoba, Minnesota and then Ontario. Undeterred the good father turned this notoriety on its head by asking anyone who came across his record walleye, genuine or not, to donate a few dollars to the Tsunami Appeal. Most have happily done so and the priest has now become known as the 'fishing father'.

ONE FOR THE POT

Sporting estates flourished during the nineteenth century, reaching their heyday prior to World War One. Rivers rich in salmon became not only the playground of the aristocracy, but also the haunt of the itinerant poacher. While the old crafty local angler taking a fish home 'for the pot' was by and large tolerated, commercially-orientated poaching gangs, often based in towns and cities, grew greatly in number.

These gangs of 'heavies' would travel to the country, armed with anything from a gun to a baseball bat, and would extract as many fish as possible and then return to the city to sell their spoils. Their often violent presence on British salmon rivers continued for at least 150 years and only lessened when the severe decline of the Atlantic salmon made much of their activities unviable.

WHICH FLY?

The range of fishing flies on the market today is quite extraordinary. What began as but a twist of fur and feather now encompasses a cast of thousands. Here are just a few:

Blobs • Bubbled sedges • Buzzers
CDC flies • Coneheads • Czech mates
Daddies • Damsels • Depth charge nymphs
Diawl bach's • Dog nobblers • Dry flies
Emergers • General purpose nymphs
Hackled wets • Hoppers • Krystal eggs
Magic circle nymphs • Mayflies
Minky boobies • Muddlers • Parachute flies
Pheasant tails • Tadpoles • Thorax flies
Traditional wets • Zonkers

MUDDLING ALONG

The ancient art of muddling is a quaint way of attracting that small but precious English fish, the gudgeon. To be executed successfully, the angler needs to acquire a newly-cut sod of earth and, thus armed, wade into the river, place the sod in a fast-flowing bit of the current and then wait a while. This ploy will send out a cloud of silty earth into the current and is said to attract gudgeon from far and wide. The angler can then catch the fish at leisure. It is thought that muddling may be the origin of the modern word mud-dle, for certainly the modern word means a clouded view.

A BIT FISHY

To what fish do these names relate?
coles, grays, coomasaham, trevelyans, blunt nosed and scharffs.
Answer on page 144.

Too many rods spoil the loch

WHAT ANGLERS SUFFER IN
THE NAME OF THEIR SUPPORT

Tangle-itus

This illness will almost invariably strike any type of angler who has just spotted the fish of a lifetime. Unfortunately, instead of casting out a delicate line to the waiting leviathan, the fisher launches out little more than a ball of knitting, and then spends the next half an hour trying to untangle it. By the time all is unpicked and well again the fish has made for cover, if not completely disappeared.

HOW FISH GOT THEIR NAMES

Char

Artic char (or charr) are a beautifully-coloured native fish featuring in deep lochs and lakes in the north of Scotland, parts of Wales and in Ireland. The fish derive their name from ancient Gaelic which denoted the fish as 'tarr-dhearg' or 'tar deargan' or even 'tarragan'. All of these spellings meant 'red bellies' or 'red fellows'. Over time the Gaelic name became corrupted into English first to char and then to charr. The English often recorded old Scots words phonetically rather than observe their true spellings. Often they would stick a double 'r' on a Scots word for emphasis or perhaps to cover up the fact they could not quite get their teeth round the soft Gaelic pronunciation of 'tar', which sounds like t-haar.

STRIPERS FOR EVER

According to www.stripersforever.org, the sea-dwelling fish the striped bass is having a bit of a hard time of it. It seems that despite its huge recreational angling popularity, the striper has never been classed as a game fish. This puts it at an immediate disadvantage when it comes to angling availability. The principal reason for this non classification appears to be to safeguard the commercial interests of the trawler fishermen. Each year the trawlermen harvest thousands of these high quality fish, selling them at a high price on the open market. According to the website, by keeping the sporting anglers interests at bay, the government effectively subsidises the jobs of the commercial fishermen. Not surprisingly the anglers case is now being more forcibly put to the powers that be with sport fishers claiming that striped bass are the 'people's fish' and that 'basic freedoms of citizenship' are at stake. Strong stuff – but then anglers do take their very sport seriously...

NECESSARIES FOR
A DAY'S BOAT FISHING

1. A well-plumped cushion
2. Balaclava-type head gear which covers neck and head
3. A baler for leaks, boat and personal
4. Bits of string, tape and bendy wire
5. Two rollocks
6. Two oars
7. A reliable outboard motor, if there is such a thing
8. Spare fuel for engine
9. Hot libations
10. A non-leaky waterproof that does not truss you up like a chicken
11. A black bin bag (sit on it, put things in it, etc)
12. An anchor with painter
13. Life jackets
14. Spare fuel for self

FISH WARS

Sold-off Senegal

For over 20 years the poverty stricken West African State of Senegal benefited from the income generated by leasing out its fishing rights. The waters off Senegal are rich in fish and EU countries snapped up the deals being offered. For a time the arrangement worked well; however the Senegalese did not reckon on the capacity for high tech trawlers to literally 'hoover up' their fish stocks, leaving locals with a greatly depleted natural resource. Little wooden skiffs and punts were no match for the huge industrial trawlers, and the battle was over before it began. In 2002 the exploitation was finally stopped, and Senegal banned EU vessels from fishing their coastal waters. Whether the fish stocks will ever recover remains to be seen.

I BELONG TO GLASGOW

Great industrial city or 'dear green place' it might be, but lesser known is the fact that Glasgow was first and foremost a salmon fishing hamlet based on the River Clyde. Within Glasgow's coat of arms is the legend:

> *There's the tree that never grew,*
> *There's the bird that never flew,*
> *There's the fish that never swam,*
> *There's the bell that never rang.*

The legend surrounding the 'fish that never swam' concerned a lost ring, given by the King of Strathclyde to his errant wife. The Queen is said to have given the ring to a knight, perhaps a secret admirer, but the King found out and crept up on the sleeping knight and took the ring back. In a fit of pique it is said he threw it into the Clyde. The next day a furious King threatened to put the Queen to death unless she brought him the ring. The gallant knight came to the rescue when he confessed to St Mungo, who dispatched a monk post-haste to the river to catch a salmon. When St Mungo cut open the fish there was the ring.

Outcome: One relieved Queen and one fish that never swam...

FISH USED IN HERALDRY

Incorporating a fish into a coat of arms has been common practice in Britain for centuries. Examples of various species seen include:

The dolphin • The trout • The grayling
The pike • The shark • The mackerel
The bream • The carp • The bream
The sparling

COMPLEATLY WALTON

When Isaak Walton wrote the seminal fishing book *The Compleat Angler* in 1653, he wanted its title to convey that the book contained quintessential knowledge of all things fishing, which of course it did. However the word 'compleat' has since fallen into disuse in the UK and has been replaced by its modern version 'complete'. Fortunately, while the Brits have let the archaic 'compleat' fall by the wayside, the Americans have embraced it into their language, and use it freely. Perhaps another case of the Americans taking something very English and making it their own...

DISAPPEARING SEA TROUT

In recent years catches of sea trout off the west coast of Scotland have fallen from being prolific in the 1960s to being a shadow of their former glory in the twenty-first century. Although we hear many theories as to their decline – anything from global warming to lack of rainfall gets a look in – it is significant that the fall in catches (in the 1980s and 1990s) coincided with the siting of large industrial fish farms in estuaries through which the sea trout must pass. Sea trout are migratory fish, and as youngsters they leave their native rivers to go to sea in order to feed and grow. However, the clouds of sea lice parasites uncontrollably emanating from the fish farms not only bother the stew pond salmon, but also have destroyed thousands if not millions of young wild sea trout. While pro and anti fish farm scientists bickered for years over whether there even was a 'lice problem' and successive governments refused to admit the fish farms were wrongly sited in the first place, the wonderful Scottish sea trout took a dreadful beating, from which it may never recover.

Do all anglers drink like the proverbial?

BUT IS IT ART?

One of the many ventures of controversial artist Damien Hirst involved a large, predatory fish. The artist obtained a 14ft tiger shark and suspended it in a glass case in a strong solution of limpid green formaldehyde. While you might be forgiven for thinking there is little artistic value in a dead fish, and a protected one at that, left mouth agape dangling forlornly in a bucket of preserving fluid, American billionaire Steven Cohen obviously saw merit in it. In 2005 he paid a cool $8 million to have Hirst's piece swimming in his own art collection.

TEN USEFUL WEBSITES

www.talkflyfishing.com
Swop fishy tales with other fishing enthusiasts.

www.coarse-fisherman.co.uk
Everything from the carp/pike/perch enthusiast.

www.sea-fishing.org
Salt water fishing, tackle, news, reviews etc.

www.fishandfly.com
Probably the longest running UK fly fishing website.

www.content-angler.com
Quirky American site explaining the
ephemeral joys of fishing.

www.flytyingforum.com
An absolute must for the avid fly-tyer.

www.fishing-highland.co.uk
Excellent site for finding out more about
fishing in the Scottish highlands.

www.anglerscircle.co.uk
A chat site where you can engage in everything
from fishy facts to fishy gossip.

www.fishingworks.com
Comprehensive info on all things fishing.

www.fishing.co.uk
Fishing articles, holidays, book reviews and more.

A BIT FISHY

Yellow, white, grey, blue, black, red are all colours that
can be used to describe which fish species? And which of
these coloured fish contains some non-European genes?
Answer on page 144.

SOLDIER PALMERS

The Soldier Palmer is a popular trout fly commonly used on many Scottish and Irish loughs. Its history could effectively stretch back to Roman times, when a Roman, Aelianus, wrote of fishing for trout with an artificial fly. It had a red body and brown feather hackle, designed in a very similar way to the later British version. Palmers were probably the first type of very basic artificial fly used to catch trout in Britain. The name Soldier Palmer appears to come from medieval times, when soldiers returning from Holy Wars wearing the uniform of the bright red cross would have (presumably brown-leaved) palms strewn at their feet.

CLOSED FOR BUSINESS

Most freshwater fish in the UK need a break away from anglers' attentions. This rest period or 'close season' is normally the allotted time that the fish have to spawn and continue the species, so by law, anglers must stop fishing and give them a break.

Here are some examples:
1. You cannot fish for coarse fish species between 15 March and 15 June.
2. You cannot fish for brown trout between 6 October and 15 March.
3. You cannot fish for salmon on the River Tweed between 30 November and 1 February.
4. You cannot fish for salmon on the River Tay between 15 October and 15 January.
5. You generally cannot fish for migratory fish (like salmon) in numerous other rivers around the UK, from mid October to early February. Check the exact local opening and closing times before you go, to avoid disappointment.

ARE YOU GOING TO
SCARBOROUGH FAIR?

Although it is almost forgotten now, Scarborough was once the haunt of leading 1930s socialites and millionaires. Just like Scotland in August, where hunters head for the grouse, Scarborough was on the elite's social calendar for its autumn sea fishing. The Rothschilds went, as did the Astors, and this quiet seaside town gained a huge reputation among the London set – quite simply, it was the place to see and be seen. However the quarry was not the North sea's humble cod or haddock; the gentry were after much bigger game – tuna. Known locally as the 'tunny', wealthy anglers flocked to catch the huge tuna, which in the early 1900s could be caught in the waters off the Scarborough coast. These big game fish came up from the Med, to feed greedily on the bounteous herring shoals to be found off England's eastern coast in

the 1930s. 'British' tuna then grew to enormous size, and eye-popping fish of 550lb to 750lb were regularly caught off these shores. From the 1930s until the outbreak of World War Two, big game anglers haunted this shoreline, the most famous of these hunters being a man-named Mitchell-Henry. Brought up on tuna fishing in Nova Scotia, he made the crossover to British tuna in 1929 and never looked back. In 1933 Mitchell-Henry caught the British record tunny, a colossal fish of 859lb. He then got into tackle design and became affiliated to that famous tackle dealer, The House of Hardy. Hardys made a special reel for him, with which to fish for tunny, called, naturally enough, the Mitchell-Henry Reel. The reel was unusually big and in ancient sepia photographs of the proud designer standing beside his enormous catch, the device looks for all the world like a small frying pan.

Mitchell-Henry was also one of the founder members of the 'British Tunny Club', an extremely pukka organisation, chock full of lords, ladies, dukes and duchesses. All had a rollicking time chasing big game at sea until war broke out and, coincidentally, the herring fisheries collapsed from over-exploitation. Without the quality of feeding to attract them to cooler northern waters, those tuna that had not been caught abruptly stopped coming up from the Med. By the 1950s the social set had deserted Scarborough as quickly as they had adopted it, and a short-lived but dramatic piece of British fishing history is now confined to a quiet corner of the Scarborough Museum.

TEN ANGLING AMERICANISMS

American fishermen have their own special language when it comes to referring to fish, tackle and assorted insects, most of which are a bit meaningless to us Brits. Below are a few quaint Americanisms explained:

Stripers	That popular sport fish, the striped bass
No see ums	Tiny insects a trout might eat
Bobbers	Small float and/or a sight indicator when fly fishing
Clousers	Type of artificial fly type, made with inverted hook and large eyes
Mayflies	All olive and mayfly species come under this collective name in America
Flavs	Insect species, full name *Flavilinea*
Crawdads	Small crayfish also known as 'mud bugs'
Hippers	Waders that reach to the hip
Freestone	A type of river with a loose stone and gravel bed
Humpy	Type of artificial fly made with deer hair body

23

BIG, BIGGER, BIGGEST FISH

You can describe your prize catch as:

A lunker
A clunker
A beauty
A denizen
A leviathan
A whopper
A specimen
A monster
One for the glass case

THE WINDOW OF OPPORTUNITY

A fish's eyeballs are not the same as ours. For a start the eyes are on the side of the head and do not have any protective eyelids or eyelashes. This means that some fish species will shy away from bright light, as they cannot blink as we do. Neither do freshwater fish see underwater in the way humans do. If you imagine you are a little trout finning away in the stream, what you actually see above you is a sort of circular window. It's actually quite a pin sharp area, but it's small; the rest of what you see are reflections from the bottom of the water surface rather like a reflection in a mirror. What the angler has to do is keep his outline out of the clear vision 'window' while getting his fly visible in the 'mirror'. It is thought that this idea of fish vision brought about different styles of angling; for example, an angler casting upstream to a fish keeps his shadow out of the 'window' because he is tucked out of sight behind his quarry. Equally, fishing a sunk (wet) fly allows the fly to pop magically through the 'mirror' and appear enticingly in front of the fish. Well, that's the theory, at least…

FLY FOLKLORE

There are many sayings associated with trout fishing, some more useful than others. Here are a few examples:

1. **Bright day, bright fly** – This is an old maxim about choosing a twinkly bright fly with silver or gold body and/or rib, on a day when there is bright sunshine. The idea is that the fish will spot something flashing in the sunlight and seize it vigorously. Verdict: sometimes works but not 100% reliable.
2. **Dull fly, dull day** – This old saying is perhaps more useful than 'bright day, bright fly'. A fish's eyesight is different from ours and fish do indeed see a dark-coloured fly against a dark sky better than the opposite. Verdict: useful ploy and fails to work only if fish are not in your vicinity anyway.
3. **Big rocks, big fish** – This old saying refers to boulders that are semi-submerged in lakes or large rivers. Trout like to use these as shelter from predators and wild weather, and the crevasses between rocks also harbour good food sources like caddis and snails. Verdict: useful but works only if the water itself is reasonably rich, rocky acidic water may not be so productive.
4. **Clear water, big fish** – Clarity of water can sometimes give a guide to the likely size of trout present. Clear water systems that are spring fed from a limestone base provide rich feeding and consequently the trout grow large. English chalkstreams are a good illustration. Verdict: helpful, but check other environmental factors as well.

A BIT FISHY

What do mackerel, dace, trout, minnow and ruffe
have in common?
Answer on page 144.

VIVE LA DIFFERENCE

That doyen of haute cuisine, Georges Auguste Escoffier, once feted the humble pike with a recipe 'Quenelles de Brochet a la Lyonnaise'. Here is the Anglicised version:

Ingredients:
1lb pike meat
1lb beef kidney fat
1lb frangipane panada
4 egg whites

Method: Fillet the pike, remove skin and bones and then pound up the flesh. Make a fish stock with the bones combined with the usual ingredients of white wine vinegar, seasoning, tarragon etc.

Pound up the kidney fat in a separate dish. Prepare panada and then mix up 1lb of this with the four beaten egg whites. Slowly combine the pike meat and the fat to the frangipane mixture and pound all to a smooth paste. Rub through a sieve until a puree with the appearance of forcemeat stuffing is obtained. Leave to cool.

Mould some quenelles from the mixture and then poach them for about seven minutes in boiling salted water. Drain and simmer in some of the fish stock for a further 10 minutes and then combine with whatever sauce you fancy.

TERRIBLE FISHING JOKES

Two anglers were chatting away as they made their way to the riverbank. 'Oh I love fishing,' said one. 'The fresh air. The solitude. The birds singing, the sunsets. It's man against nature, pitting your wits with denizens of the deep. The thrill of catching a fish and the battle to land a crafty adversary. Tell me. Why do you go fishing?'

'My daughter's learning to play the violin.'

OPEN WIDE!

It's often said that the pike is the shark of the freshwater world. Certainly he's a greedy predator, eating anything he can wrap his jaws around. Pike grow to huge sizes – specimens up to 19 kilos have been caught in Britain and there are probably larger ones lurking. Pike have been known to devour anything from rats and birds to water voles and trout. Tales abound of the pike's voracity. One of the best is from the *Fishing Gazette* written by H Band in 1883: 'A few paces below me I noticed three young sand martins perched on a bough, which overhung the water. They could hardly fly, and the old ones were fluttering about them. My float lay motionless on the surface. Suddenly there was a tremendous splash in the water directly down under the withie bough, which swung up and down. One bird was still on the bough, and another, after fluttering about a little, again settled down on it. I looked on in amazement; the waves, caused by the splash, spread over the river, the surface became smooth and still again, but one bird was missing.

'A bite at my line recalled my attention to fishing; but presently there was another splash under the bough, which swayed about again – the other bird was missing, and now only one remained, balancing itself with difficulty on the swinging branch. That the thief was a pike was quite evident. I stuck my rod-butt into the soft bank, and quietly approached the spot, soon finding a convenient place from which to reconnoitre. Steadily I watched for a long time. The final dash of the pike occurred so violently, so suddenly – and this time from the side where I had been sitting – that I could only get an instants view of what had happened. The third sand martin was gone. The swaying bough grew still again and all was over.'

BE KIND TO YOUR CATCH

In coarse fishing the (largely inedible) catch is almost always released after being weighed and photographed. In sea fishing some fish are put back after recording their size, while some good eating species like cod or mackerel are kept. Game fishing is different. Some fisheries operate a 'catch and release' rule, usually in the name of conservation of particular endangered species like Atlantic salmon. This means fish have to be returned alive and kicking. Here's how to be kind to your catch:

1. Use a knotless net which does not rub the delicate protective mucous of the back of the fish.
2. Use a rod and line fit for the job. Avoid playing heavy fish to a standstill on flimsy tackle.
3. Wet your hands before handling the fish.
4. If you want a photograph, keep the fish in the landing net in the water, lift from there, quick snap and back she goes into the net and from there into the stream.
5. Keep all fish out of the water for as short a time as possible.
6. When releasing a big fish, face it head on into the current, hold gently by the tail and allow the fish to get its gills going before letting it go. The days of 'throw it back' are long gone.
7. Similarly in lake fishing, hold the fish under the water by the tail and work it gently back and forth until it kicks and scoots off.
8. Using a barbless hook is sometimes compulsory. This allows the fish to be slipped off easily from the hook.

A BIT FISHY

Where would you find a *Cristivomer namaycush*
(and no, this is not an anagram)?
Answer on page 144.

MACNABBING

A 'Macnab' is a highland sporting challenge of shooting a grouse, catching a salmon and killing a stag all in the one day. The custom is believed to have begun after John Buchan wrote his classic novel *John Macnab*. While in the early 1900s a Macnab was relatively easy to achieve, today's scarcity of wild game makes the challenge an almost impossible one, with a considerable modicum of luck involved. Frequently, sportsmen will have little difficulty nabbing the stag and the grouse but have their ambitions confounded by the lack of Atlantic salmon in Scotland rivers. Either that or they will hook a fish first thing, shoot the stag and then find the grouse have all shown a clean pair of heels and winged it over on to a neighbouring inaccessible moor.

TRADING PLAICES

According to a report in *The Times*, fish are now a global commodity like oil or gold. Gone are the days when consumers contented themselves with Friday's little bit of haddock or cod. Today's customers want tuna, grouper, sea bream, snapper or swordfish. Demand for exotic seafood has also now reached an all-time high and sea fishermen have had to go hi-tech to keep up. According to the report, fishermen use live web cams or mobile phone photography at sea to email pictures of their latest catches to waiting fish dealers who bid online for the fish. Effectively this means a fish caught in the Indian Ocean can be bought at sea, landed, processed by the fish buyer, shipped on ice by plane, zoomed to Billingsgate market, resold through your local fish shop and cooked to perfection by your fair hand, all in the space of two days. Phew!

MAYFLY

'The Mayfly is up!' is a shout that will send trout anglers scuttling from pub to riverbank at a superior rate of knots. Quite simply this is 'the' time to go trout fishing. The usually cautious fish let down their guard while trying to gulp down as many of these protein-packed insects as possible and can be caught relatively easily. Often you will see the few weeks of the mayfly season described as 'Duffers Fortnight' and that about sums it up. British mayflies are also known as green drakes and, with their delicate lace-like translucent wings, they are really quite beautiful. Although they are given the name 'Mayfly', the bulk of the insect hatch occurs in June, and depending in which neck of the British woods you hang out, the hatch may last anything from two weeks to two months. Although it is normally assumed that mayfly prefer to inhabit only English chalk streams, the flies are much more widespread and are found in numerous northern lochs, particularly those of Caithness and Sutherland.

It is often thought that this much-prized insect requires alkaline water to thrive, but the presence of clay-like mud in the river or lake, firm enough for the mayfly nymph to make a decent burrow for its home, is actually more important. Here the nymph may live for up to two years before rising up through the water. Then with a dramatic splitting of the nymph shuck, finally the adult emerges, struggles for a moment on the surface, as if gasping for air, and then takes flight to the nearest vegetation. The mayfly then spends perhaps two days on land drying its wings, during which time the males will dance in spectacular columns in the hope of attracting a female to mate in their midst.

Ultimately after two long years in a dark burrow and two short days carousing, the mayfly mate, the female sheds her eggs back into the water and the delicate Romeo and Juliets die, falling spent with wings splayed, back on to the water from whence they came. While all this drama is in progress, hungry but incautious trout lay themselves open to attack, especially from the cunning angler who imitates the insects with clever designs of natural fly. It is no accident that fishing fans call this hive of activity the mayfly carnival, a madly exciting time for both anglers and fish.

OLD PISCATORIALS – NEW EDITORIALS

Take me to the river...

FAMOUS LADIES IN FISHING

Princess Grace of Monaco

In the 1950s and early 1960s, the late Princess Grace was a renowned angler and madly keen on coarse fishing. Her exploits were rarely recorded however, as she would fish incognito away from the prying paparazzi, disguised as an elderly stooped crone. Only a privileged few ever knew who it really was participating on the open match circuit, where she was highly adept at whizzing out a mean swim feeder and bagging double nets of 'dustbin lids' – large bream to you and me.

BEFORE NYLON WAS INVENTED

In order to keep the fish from seeing and being spooked by the thick part of the fishing line, some form of tapered leader (the bit that joins hook to line) had to be made onto which would be attached the hook or fly. Fishing lines dating from the 1400s had their own in-built leader and were made from braided horsehair tapered down to a fine semi-invisible single strand of hair at the end of which would be the hook. These were neat and beautifully-made contraptions, but required careful attention otherwise they would snap. During the nineteenth century horsehair lines were replaced by silk lines, and then gut, which would be tied on at the end of the line to form the leader. The first gut was made from the entrails of a silkworm and later, until silk became scarcer, and then sheep's intestines provided a cheaper alternative. Whatever the type of gut, it still needed a huge amount of care. It had to be kept damp in order to avoid britleness. All in all, anglers breathed a collective sigh of relief when the nylon leader was invented in the 1930s, and have never looked back.

MAGIC MERMAIDS

Hallucinations (drink-induced or not), sleep deprivation, sexual frustration and poor eyesight seem to be at the root of stories connected with those mythical creatures, the mermaids. Let's face it, if you are a fisherman on board a trawler, spending long and arduous days and nights at sea, there may well come a time when you start pining for the company of a beautiful woman, and see things that aren't really there. So it's not surprising that tales of mermaids, with supernatural powers abound from one length of the country to the other. At Mermaids Rock on the far eastern tip of Cornwall, fishermen are said to have been lured to a watery grave by the sound of singing mermaids. At the other end of the country, fish-tailed damsels are supposed to haunt the rocks of Sandwood Bay on the western shores of North Sutherland. And their eerie presence is not confined to the sea. Black Mere, in inland Staffordshire is said to be haunted by a strange mermaid, as is the pool on Kinder Downfall in Derbyshire. In Scotland, the plunging Corrie Halloch gorge in Wester Ross is also linked to a spooky lady not unlike a mermaid. Exhausted, lonely and tipsy fishermen certainly have a lot to answer for…

ALL AT SEA

While sea fishing, you can employ any or all of the following:

Bullets • Legers • Jigs
Multipliers • Paternosters
Pendulums • Rigs • Shock leaders
Stop knots • Swivels

FISHY FIGURES

145

Number of salmon passing through the Waddow fish
counter on the River Ribble in May 2003

LONGEST (FISHING) BOOK TITLE EVER?

In 1658 Richard Franck wrote *Northern Memoirs*,
which was finally published in 1694 when the publisher
had collected enough ink. The full title runs as follows:

Northern Memoirs
Calculated for the
Meridian of Scotland

Wherein most of the Cities, Citadels,
Sea Ports, Castles, Forts, Fortresses
Rivers, and Rivulets, are compendiously
described

Together with choice Collections of various Discoveries,
Remarkable Observations, Theological
Notions, Political Axioms, National Intrigues,
Polemick Inferences, Contemplations, Speculations,
and several curious and industrious Inspections,
lineally drawn from Antiquaries, and
other noted and intelligible Persons of Honour
and Eminency

To which is added:

The Contemplative and Practical Angler
By way of a diversion. With a Narrative of that dextrous
and mysterious Art experimented in England, and
perfected in more remote and solitary Parts of Scotland.
By way of Dialogue.

It was not a best seller.

SHARKS AIN'T FUSSY

According to VM Coppleson who wrote *Shark Attack* in 1959, the following have been found in sharks' stomachs:

Three overcoats
One fully grown spaniel with collar
Several legs of mutton
Large piece of sacking
Head and forelegs of a bulldog
One nylon raincoat
One porpoise skull
Half a ham
Numerous sea birds
Numerous fish
Hind quarter of a pig
Assorted porcupine spines
Several lumps of horse flesh
One driving licence

HOW FISH GOT THEIR NAMES

Bream

Bream are silvery, iridescent freshwater fish with either bluish or brownish backs that can be found in lakes and slow-going rivers all over the world. Many examples of 'sea-bream' also exist, their family name *Sparidae* accounting for at least 40 species in the globe's more exotic climes. It is likely that these tropical bream were named for much the same reason as their freshwater brethren – because of their spectacular lustrous scales. From the proto-Germanic base word 'brehwan' meaning 'to shine, glitter or sparkle', came the West Germanic 'brasm', before being lengthened to the Frankish 'brahisma', and then shortened again to the Old French 'bresme' – the word from which its current pronunciation is derived.

A NORMAN INVASION

It is likely that the very first anglers in Britain came from Western Europe, probably during the Norman Invasion. The Normans arrived bearing not only arms but also fishing rods, which the English later deemed to call in their uniquely convoluted way 'angles'. Actually the word 'angle' originally referred to the bend in a fishing hook, somehow it got transferred to the rod and then finally to the man using it. Hence anything loosely to do with fishing became known as 'angling'. The first fishing rods were little more than long poles, and reels did not come into use until the 1600s. It is not thought the Normans invented rod fishing *per se*, but they may have procured the idea from Mediterranean countries where the 'Bolognese' rod was and still is, in common use. These rods, up to 20 foot or so, were the most basic of bait rods; all the angler needed to do was extend the rod over the water and dangle in the line and baited hook in the hope of attracting dinner. It seems that the Normans not only created war widows but also fishing widows.

SUPERSTITIONS OF THE SEAFARERS

On the wind

In Caithness in northern Scotland, sea fishermen of yore had deep superstitions concerning wind or rather that some person wishing them ill could 'whistle up the wind'. The wife of a Caithness fisherman would never blow on any food to cool it down, as it was thought she would cause a storm to rise and endanger her man out at sea. Every time a storm blew up it was presumably 'her at home's' fault and the seafarers would turn to one another with the desperate cry: 'She's made those cakes again!'.

BRITAIN'S FISHING FASHIONS

Scottish wets

Scotland may often be wet and windy but it's also the traditional home of what is known as wet fly fishing. Wet flies are the ones that sink below the water surface and Scots have fished with these patterns since the nation first embraced the art of fly fishing in the nineteenth century, if not earlier. This method of fishing suits the Scottish temperament to a tee; canny, searching and methodical. When executed skillfully, wet fly fishing on river and loch thoroughly covers all angles and depths. Few trout can resist the lure of a well-presented wet Dunkeld, Clan Chief or Loch Ordie, flies not quite with kilts on but close enough.

NICKNAMES FOR FISH

Barse – perch
Cuddy – freshwater Artic char
Haddies – haddock
Silver darlings – herring

ENTER THE ROBOTIC FISH

Professor Jens Blachen of the Norwegian University of Science and Technology at Trondheim has come up with a novel remote controlled 'cyberfish' which is going to give us an inside view of the problems fish are facing in the world's oceans. The device literally swims with the fish in their unique shoals and relays its data electronically. Apparently Professor Balchens team have so far learned that regarding navigation and avoiding predators, salmon are distinctly dim, cod are stubborn and difficult to steer but the humble coley (saithe) is by far the smartest of the subjects tested so far.

LONG ISLAND ON THE LINE

Anglers and commercial fishermen of Long Island Sound, off the eastern seaboard of America are up in arms at the prospect of a huge floating liquid gas terminal being set in the midst of their fish-rich waters. According to the website www.savethesound.org, the area is one of the most important bodies of water in the USA. It is home to thousands of species of wildlife and fish and provides employment and recreational opportunities for millions of people. Should the development get the go-ahead the area will be transformed with a 10 storey terminal the length of four football pitches. Fishermen will also have their access cut dramatically in the area not to mention the potential for pollution from the plant. Environmentalists claim the facility will threaten human and ecological safety; developers say it will do no such thing. With no common ground anywhere it looks as if this argument will run and run.

REASONS TO GO FISHING

Anglers can always come up with an excuse to go fishing. Here are some of the better ones:

- You are engaged in research into fish species.
- The freezer is empty.
- You need fresh air.
- You just know you will catch that monster you missed last time.
- The pensioner next door has run out of fish.
- The dog needs the exercise.
- You want to test a new rod/reel/line/fly (rotate choice accordingly).
- You have an overwhelming desire to wear old clothes and truss yourself up in neoprene.
- Fishing is your hydrotherapy and anyway it's a lot cheaper than the spa.

DON'T FORGET YOUR PARACHUTE

According to the *Oxford English Dictionary* a parachute is an apparatus used to check a fall through air and/or descend safely from a great height. When fishing, anglers can use flies made with parachute hackles, which do a similar thing to the descent of a fly as it is cast on to the water. The idea is to tie on feather hackle in such a way that, when finished, the fly looks as if it has its own little personal umbrella attached. The origin of this style of fly tying is obscure, possibly American or Scottish depending on which camp you believe. However English anglers Goddard and Clarke took the design one step further when they made 'upside down' parachute flies. This had the little umbrella parachute on the underside of the hook and, upon landing on the water, the hook point sat up above the water surface. The concept behind this was to fool the trout by keeping the sharp end out of sight. Whether the trout ever noticed this extra subtlety is not known.

BRITAIN'S FISHING FASHIONS

England's elegant dries

While their neighbours adopted practical approaches to their fishing, the English for a time allowed themselves to be swept away in a tidal wave of fishing fashion. When the dry fly, a fly that floats on the water surface, was first popularised in the late nineteenth century, England's fishing glitterati deemed it to be the height of angling elegance. For a time any other method was frowned upon, if not banned. Gentlemen of the Shires used 'dray flay', ruffians and rogues did not. As with many trends in social snobbery, it took two world wars to put the fashion of the immaculately dressed mayfly back in perspective.

I did say, cast your net in the water…

FOODY FLIES

Shrimps

While salmon are at sea they are very partial to the odd shrimp. In fact, eating these crustaceans gives their flesh that rich orange-red tone, whereas a diet without lots of shrimp means that the salmon's flesh remains a dull grey-white. Salmon anglers realised this quite some years ago and tied flies that vaguely resembled a darting shrimp, in the hope that seeing the gaudy fly in a river would remind the salmon of their sea-feeding phase. In the 1980s Scotsman Ally Gowans invented a British, if not world, bestselling salmon fly known as 'The Ally's Shrimp'. This fly has a brilliant orange and black hue and has proved irresistible to salmon everywhere.

FISHY FIGURES

109

Average length, in millimetres, of the ruffe in the UK

SIX GOOD REASONS TO EAT MORE FISH

1. Fish contain omega-3 oils, which are known to assist in the prevention of heart disease and strokes. Consumers who eat fish regularly ie at least twice a week, tend to have fewer heart attacks and strokes. All fish is good, however, providing they all come from a sustainable source, fresh tuna, herring, mackerel, mullet and salmon are all especially high in that magic ingredient omega-3.

2. Fish are low in the 'bad' saturated fats. The healthiest ways to cook your fish are by steaming, grilling or baking. Fish that is deep fried in thick batter (as most fish suppers are) is delicious but loses its important low-fat qualities. Pity.

3. Fish are good for your bones. Canned fish like sardine and salmon contain softened edible bones, which are said to add to your calcium levels. A glass of milk with a plate of steamed fresh fish might have a similar effect.

4. Fish is good for diabetes sufferers. Since those with diabetes are at greater risk from heart disease, a diet containing lots of fish will help lessen that risk.

5. Fish can aid in the treatment of asthmatics. Research suggests that children who eat fish regularly are less likely to develop asthma.

6. Fish are comparatively inexpensive. You can derive as much nutritional benefit from a fresh mackerel as you can from beef mince, with the added bonus you do not consume as much saturated fats.

CATCHING THE COELACANTH

Unlike the Loch Ness monster whose presence has never advanced beyond the realms of myth and mystery, the coelacanth (pronounced 'sealakanth') has been caught and confirmed as one of the world's few remaining living fossils. Its origins have been traced back some 400 million years. With its limb-like fins and luminescent eyes, it is thought that the coelacanth was one of the first fish to crawl out of the sea and on to land. On becoming land-based, the species slowly evolved, first into reptiles, then mammals and finally, a long way down the ecological ladder, mankind itself.

SUPERSTITIONS OF THE SEAFARERS

Blood and guts

Sailors are notoriously superstitious. When going fishing off the north east coast of Scotland, the men of Morayshire regarded it as unlucky to begin the season before blood had been shed. Wishing any seaman 'Have a good trip' was desperately unlucky if he had not seen blood spilt before you gave him your best. Often fist-fights would be started in order to render this fresh blood. Fishermen of Portlessie, in north east Scotland would punch the nose of anyone silly enough to wish them 'bon voyage', thus dispelling lurking demons by immediately drawing blood. Onboard boat it was apparently also considered bad luck not to 'take blood' from the first fish to come up over the side. What the sailors did with the blood is anyone's guess.

A BIT FISHY

Name six species of fish ending in '-ing'.
Answer on page 144.

SALMON AND SASSENACHS –
SHOW US YOUR GOLD

In 1429 the ninth parliament of James I passed an Act which detailed various measures on salmon preservation. However, written into its midst was a distinct bias towards the Scottish fish merchants of this era. The Act stated 'It is ordained that no Scottish man sell to Englishmen, or in England beforehand or otherwaies, ony salmonde, bot that Englishmen bye them in Scotland for English gold, and none other contentation.'

It then went on to advocate that if the English would not buy Scottish salmon in Scotland that 'the Scottish merchandes may sell them in Flanders or other places, quhair them thinkis; swa that of wise they nouther send them nor sell them in England.' Thus James I ensured that the English would always have to travel to Scotland to buy their salmon and thereby probably created one of the first monopoly fish markets in Britain.

PASS THE PROP

Fishing on Australia Day in 2003, an Australian trawler netted the catch of the year when it connected with a huge propeller from a 1940s naval plane. Fishing in their usual spot 14 miles off Ulladulla, the crew of the Arakiwa were astonished when an old propeller came to the surface. Although badly rusted, the propeller still had its five blades attached and the curling at the wing tips showed the force at which the original plane hit the water. The catch proved a costly exercise. It took the trawler a full four hours to get back to port, the tangled net cost AUS$8,000 to replace and the crew had to hire a crane to get their unusual catch out of the water.

CAUGHT AND RELEASED

Since the 1960s, when stocks of game fish such as wild salmon began to seriously diminish, there has been an ongoing dilemma in the sport of game fishing. It involves killing (or not, as the case may be). On the one hand anglers like to see themselves as skilled hunters stalking their prey as our ancestors did. We learn skills that allow us to land the fly inches from the salmon's nose, we spend long hours studying watercraft and getting to know about the habits of fish. We make shedloads of mistakes but eventually we learn enough from our experiences to be able to really know what we are doing. Then we creep up along the river, select a likely spot, launch a handmade fly so convincing that a salmon takes a pop at it and, bingo, we have the catch. All our inherited genes tell us we should bear the prize home for our family to admire and more importantly to eat. We are proud of our achievements in providing food for the home, and rightly so.

The antithesis of this behaviour is the modern ethos that, having struggled sometimes for years to catch your prized wild salmon, you should then put it back. Anglers call this 'Catch and Release', and of all the fishing methods this is presently one of the most controversial. The aim is undoubtedly laudable – having caught the salmon, you return it to the wild to go on and continue the species. But many anglers think this a weak conservation measure, put in place only after centuries of overfishing by other people. The trouble is that salmon fishing was and still is big business. Many anglers feel that if river fishery owners had not allowed so much over-exploitation in the past of salmon at sea and in the river, then today's angler probably wouldn't have to throw back his catch of a lifetime. The

44

other argument is that you can buy farmed salmon over the counter so cheaply that you don't need to take a fresh wild salmon home as food. Which is fine if you don't mind eating fish that often has all the excitement of a flaccid and greasy piece of rubber.

So it seems that modern game anglers are now paying the price for others' past greed, and the proud hunter is now confined to the fishing minority.

TOP TEN SALMON FLIES

All salmon anglers have their favourite flies – the ones they swear by when all else fails:

Allies shrimp	Silver doctor
Blue charm	Stoats tail
Garry dog	Thunder and lightning
General practitioner	Thunder stoat
Munro killer	Waddingtons

FISH TO CATCH FISH

In the sea virtually all fish will eat other fish, and a considerable number of species can be caught by using smaller fish as bait. Probably the best-known type of fish for this ploy is the mackerel, which, with its pungent oily smell and durability when cut in strips, makes it an ideal bait for pollack, saithe, dogfish and conger eel. Freshwater anglers in the Northern isles use strips of mackerel to tempt sea trout in brackish water. This they use on fly rod and floating line, casting the bait forward with a roll cast and then drawing the silvery slice quickly back towards them as if it were a small fleeing fish. Sand eel, whitebait, herring and squid are also used as bait cut to appropriate sizes and carefully threaded on hooks to avoid being lost. These baits are more often used on a spinning rod with multiplier reel rather than a fly rod.

What do you mean the prawns are off?

WAYS TO RUIN THE CATCH

1. Store in a plastic bag on a hot day.
2. Forget to gut it when you arrive home.
3. Leave it out uncovered overnight for the cat to nibble.
4. Boil for half an hour in unsalted water with guts in.
5. Boil for same length of time with guts out.
6. Microwave full power for 30 minutes.
7. Any combination of the above.

124

Weight, in grammes, of a nine-foot Scott fly rod

STUFF THE FISH

These days taxidermy of fish is usually done by taking an exact fibreglass mould of the catch and then having it expertly painted to resemble the real thing. This is a lot simpler than all that mess with formaldehyde; however, anglers wishing to preserve that 'fish of a lifetime' need to observe some ground rules. First it's important to take pictures of the fish to record its natural colour for reference by the artist. Fading and discoloration happens quickly once the fish is landed and exposed to the air, so , take snaps from all angles and then cover the fish. A canvas bag wetted inside and then layered with a little wet sphagnum moss is best, but use a wetted plastic bag if needs must.

To ensure the best taxidermy possible for your prize, phone ahead to ask someone to clear a space in the freezer, leave the water at speed and race home. For future reference by the taxidermist, it's advisable to note down a few essential measurements like overall length and circumference of girth. That done, place the fish flat in the freezer still in its cover but without the sphagnum moss which can freeze to the skin and damage it. Next get on the phone to your friendly fish preserver who will quote you an exorbitant fee, every bit as heart racing as the capture of the fish. Before agreeing, make sure the price includes proper post and packaging.

With any luck several weeks, or months, later the fish is returned to you in exquisitely painted fibreglass form ready to be forever admired on the study wall.

GOLDFISH DIPPER NETS
A LIFETIME BAN

The Japanese sport of goldfish dipper catching was shaken to the core in 2003 when it was discovered that its national champion had been cheating. Competition is intense in this quaint sport, and around two thousand individual competitors take part in the national event. The idea is to scoop up as many goldfish as possible in three minutes from a small pond. Competitors have to use an officially sanctioned dipper made of rice paper, rather than nylon net. This they must choose in advance from a selection shown to them by the judges. It seems the cheating competitor sneaked in his own dipper made of standard net rather than soggy rice paper and thereby won all the titles in a clean sweep. He was only found out by chance when a spectator played back a video he had made of the proceedings. The cheat had hidden the offending device behind a handheld fan, feigning trouble with the heat but actually effecting a dipper swap when he thought no one was looking.

When confronted with the evidence, the goldfish-catching superstar admitted the crime. He was stripped of his title, lost out on an all-expenses-paid trip to Hawaii and was banned from taking part in the competition for life. The Chairman of the National Goldfish Dipper Catching Federation said: 'We want to try and make the competition as fair as possible, so that we don't destroy children's dreams.'

A BIT FISHY

Which is the odd one out?
Bustard, bittern, landrail, grouse and dotterel.
Answer on page 144.

EIGHT INVALUABLE FISHING BOOKS

1. *An Angler's Entomology* by JR Harris
2. *Freshwater Fishes in Britain* by Davies, Shelley et al.
3. *Natural History of the Highlands & Islands* by Fraser Darling and JM Boyd
4. *The Trout* by W Frost and M Brown
5. *A Dictionary of Fly Fishing* by C McCully
6. *Freshwater Fishing* by Falkus and Buller
7. *The Magic Wheel* edited by Profumo and Swift
8. *The Fly* by Andrew Herd

ICE ICE BABY

You might think that sitting on ice in the middle of a great frozen lake in the wilds of Alaska or Scandinavia, waiting for a fish to bite, borders on the unusual if not a bit weird. But then, given that most fishermen and women are slightly mad anyway, this branch of angling should come as no surprise. The fish most anglers are after are usually char or walleye pollack and some big ones at that. Anglers use specially made, tiny fishing rods no more than two feet long, and after drilling a hole in the ice, they then dangle line and bait down in the hope a passing fish will take hold.

There is no casting or bait selection skill required; the most successful anglers are the ones who know where to drill their holes. Expert ice anglers pinpoint fish under the water by methodically drilling test bores around potentially productive areas, such as underwater promontories, or where they know a stream would normally flow in to the lake. In fact the drilling is much more energetic than the fishing itself which is more or less static, and usually jolly sociable with anglers passing round the beer, whisky or schnapps as they wait for a bite. Scotch on the rocks, anyone?

THE WORLD'S MOST CAUGHT FISH
AND WHO EATS THEM

Peruvian anchovy – 7.2 million tonnes of this prolific little fish, also known as the Peruvian anchoveta, were landed in 2001. Mainly caught in subtropical waters where it swims in massive shoals and feeds mainly on plankton. With this tonnage, that's a heck of a lot of pizza garnish.

Walleye pollack – Found in Alaskan waters, this is a long-living hardy fish surviving up to 15 years in its native waters if not harvested first. Considered one of the most important of the world's fish resources, around 3.1 million tonnes were caught by commercial netsmen in 2001 with a lot of the catch exported to the Japanese and Chinese sector.

Chilean jack mackerel – If you buy tinned mackerel in the UK with or without an accompanying sticky sauce, the chances are you will be eating this fish. About 2.5 million tonnes of the little critters were harvested from the south Pacific where they feed harmlessly on small shellfish and fish larvae.

FISHING FOR MARK TWAIN

According to the Missouri State Parks Department, ice fishing in the depths of winter on the 18,000-acre Mark Twain Lake is not advised due to fluctuating water levels, as well as variable ice thickness. However, when the lake is not frozen, visiting anglers can enjoy fishing for a wide variety of fish including largemouth bass, carp, bluegill, walleye, catfish and the delightfully named crappie. If you don't come prepared with your own boat for the Mark Twain water, you can conveniently move over to the Tom Sawyer Lake for some bank fishing. There is no mention of the 'Huckleberry Finn River' being available yet, but they're working on it.

I SPY

You might at first be at a loss to see the connection between a World War Two subterfuge aid and a device employed in the gentle art of trout fishing. It seems that British and American agents employed silent one-man floatation devices to creep out and spy on and/or sabotage enemy ships. These floats were rather like large rubber rings complete with an interior canvas seat. The agent would don fins and a wet suit, sit in the middle of the ring, put any gear he needed to keep dry on its raised surface or 'apron' and then paddle quietly out on the water toward the enemy. In the 1980s American manufacturers revived the idea, only this time the angler was the hunter and the quarry a wary trout. Anglers using these devices called float tubes, U-boats or belly boats, look rather akin to a very large duck. Nevertheless, float tubes remain a practical silent mode of water transport, avoiding the need for hiring boats and outboards while allowing the angler to creep up on the unsus- pecting fish.

HOW NOT TO DESCRIBE YOUR FISHING ROD

The fishing world is full of double entendres, especially when you try and converse about rods. Here are a few examples of how not to discuss the merits of a rod:

1. 'Mine's bigger than yours.'
2. 'I like a stiff one.'
3. 'Does it extend any further?'
4. 'You've got a big butt there.'
5. 'It's got male-female spigots.'
6. 'Your butt's a bit slippery.'

COMPLETELY BIASED LIST OF
WONDERFUL FISHING WRITERS

Harry Plunket Greene –
Plunket did most of his
fishing on the Hampshire
chalkstreams, notably the
River Bourne during the
1920s. He was an accom-
plished professional singer
as well as a master of the
printed word, capable of
making fishing seem witty,
beautiful and intriguing all
at the same time. His book
Where Bright Waters Meet
was written in between
his operatic recitals and
can be read again and
again without boredom.

Hugh Falkus – Falkus
was a forthright character
well known in twentieth
century angling circles for
suffering few fools gladly,
yet his angling writing
manages to combine
boundless practical insight
with grace and wit. His
heyday of fishing was in
the 1970s when he made
the English border Esk
River his own. When not
fishing, Falkus made TV
documentaries principally

on animal behaviour and
natural history and it is
his voice narrating classic
wildlife programmes such
as *The World About Us*
and *The Undersea World
of Jacques Cousteau*.

TC Kingsmill Moore –
the late KM was an
esteemed judge in the
Irish High Court and this
is only too apparent in his
writing, which was sharply
observant and astute yet
completely without
verbosity. His fishing
career spanned more than
50 years from the 1920s to
the 1970s and his book *A
Man May Fish* is probably
the best on Irish sea trout
fishing ever written.

GM Skues – Skues was
a successful barrister of
the late nineteenth century
who eagerly applied his
shrewd analysing skills
to trout angling. His far
thinking 'nymph' fishing
theories were mainly
conducted on the chalk-

streams of Hampshire and these formed a backdrop to his taking on the might of Halford's dry fly establishment. This was a prolonged and at times vicious 'wet versus dry fly' argument, spanning 20 years or more. Skues eventually won the day while still managing to write lyrically and without bitterness on the sport he loved so much.

John Inglis Hall –
Inglis Hall is a writer in the Plunket Greene mode, gently funny yet involving and inspiring. He became passionate about the remote River Truim in the wild highlands of Scotland fishing it ardently from the early 1950s. The result was *Fishing a Highland Stream – A Love Affair with a River*, a timeless work and a sheer joy to read.

FILMS WITH SOMETHING FISHY IN THEM

A Fish called Wanda
Free Willy
Little Mermaid
Shark Tale

MOST EXCITING FIGHTS ON THE RIVER

1. Play a plastic bag for half an hour in fast water.
2. Wrestle with a small bale of chicken wire, which trundles along on the bottom, in an oddly slow rotation.
3. Play a waterlogged dead sheep to a standstill.
4. Catch the push bar of a supermarket trolley.
5. Snag your lure in the laces of an old boot, size eight upwards for greatest excitement.
6. Snag your lure in the lace of an old boot still on a corpse.
7. Catch a fertiliser bag on one side near its neck so it opens and closes in the current, guaranteed to work you to exhaustion.

FINDING THE GARDEN FLY

The 'garden fly' is a coy way of describing the earthworm, an excellent bait for stubborn, sulking fish. To extract worms quickly from unlikely looking soil – for example, a garden lawn – pour slightly warm, but not hot soapy water (water for the dishes containing a dose of washing up liquid is best) over a reasonable area and wait for about three to five minutes. The worms will magically appear at the surface and it is an easy exercise to pick them off and store them in a plastic container, with some fresh moss ready for use. It seems that the earthworm has a strong dislike for soap and comes up to the surface to escape it. Just don't tell everyone who told you this tip!

WHAT ANGLERS SUFFER IN
THE NAME OF THEIR SPORT

Floatitus

This is an odd affliction of the coarse fisher. Take a look at your local canal on a Saturday and there will be many anglers there, struck down in their prime with floatitus. Symptoms for this ailment include an inability to move their eyes in any direction other than staring at the little float bobbing around in front of them. Even when engaged in deep conversation, lighting a cigarette or pouring out coffee their eyes remain transfixed.

FISHY FIGURES

41

Minimum legal length, in centimetres, of a sea bass caught on the UK shoreline, as recorded in the book *Freshwater Fishes in Britain*

BRITAIN'S FISHING FASHIONS

Dapper Irish

While their fishing brothers across the Irish Sea pussy-footed around with delicately tied exact imitations of real flies, the Irish got straight to the point, saving a bundle on fur and feather and by sticking live insects (usually mayflies) on the hook. After all, why bother with fiddly dressings when there are so many natural bugs flying about? These 'baits' were and still are fished by a method known as dapping. This involves a huge rod of about 18 feet and a line of dapping floss with a smidgeon of nylon on the end, on to which you tie the hook and its wriggly occupants. No casting is involved, you simply hoick the rod up to the perpendicular and then let the wind blow the fly and line out so that it dips enticingly on the water. With any luck, a fish sees this bunch of insects bobbing about and comes up to nab them before they disappear again.

A FEARSOME GAFF

To non-fishers, making a 'gaffe' means making a blunder. There is no mistake however, about using a 'gaff' during the course of a fishing day. This piece of fishing equipment is a mean-looking long-handled hook with a needle sharp point. It is used to scoop up a fish caught by line, and at one time was commonly used by gillies to haul out heavy salmon from the river after the angler had played them to a standstill. While in big game fishing notably in the Caribbean, the gaff is still used if the species is worth keeping for its prize winning and/or eating qualities, thankfully in the UK we use more humane methods to land fish. In England and Wales (though not Scotland) the practice of gaffing fish is now banned on all waters.

A PINCH OF CARP

Carp in the UK have now become such a designer fishing item that they attract the unwarranted attentions of specialist thieves. Big fish are being stolen almost to order, as resale on the black market can net the unscrupulous a very tidy sum. Large carp of 25lb and upward are quite rare in England and can now command prices of thousands, rather than hundreds, of pounds sterling. The English Environment Agency has advised lake owners to photographs their prize fish so that they can be identified later if they ever resurface in someone else's pond. A case of, could all carp smile please, for their own safety.

NICKNAMES FOR FISH

Culle – bullhead
Fluke – flounder
Pope – ruffe
Sellacks – young cod or saithe

ABATE A BAIT

If you have ever wondered whether the term 'bated breath' fits into angling terminology, the simple answer is, it doesn't. Despite the similar sound to that of a baited hook, the term stems from the word abate meaning lessen or reduce. Somewhere along the line the 'a' of abate was dropped and the word 'bate' was born. Shakespeare apparently used it in the *The Merchant of Venice* – 'With bated breath and whisp'ring humbleness'. Over time, the word bate fell into disuse and it is now common to understand bated breath as meaning 'reduced' breathing. In effect, holding on to your breath rather than a fishing rod…

Oh, oh, there's that bailiff again...

SUSTAINABILITY AND ALL THAT

Environmentalists are forever telling us that we need a sustainable this and a sustainable that. In fact this buzz word is applied to just about anything animal, mineral or vegetable and of course, it's applied to fisheries as well. So just what is a sustainable fishery? In truth, it is sometimes not that easy to distinguish good from bad, but the conservation-minded angler might want note the following:

A sustainable fishery is one where:
- The management and staff know and care about their fish; you'd be surprised how many do not.
- Clear records of catches, including size and weight, are kept.
- Future stocking is planned well ahead.
- Clear records of fishing effort, ie how long it took the angler to catch anything, are kept.
- Fishing methods are regulated.
- The fish you catch show a good spread of sizes from babies through to leviathans; all one size is not necessarily a healthy sign.

ALASKAN ALEUT ALERT

For over 6,000 years the remote Aleut tribe of North Alaska have survived by fishing for the sockeye salmon. They even have the archaeological evidence to prove it. Recent research has unearthed over 300 ancient village sites linking a prosperous community thriving off the proceeds of salmon harvesting. However, this traditional way of life was placed under threat in 2005 when the Aleut were told by US environmental groups and the North Pacific Fishery Management Council to cease fishing as they were 'damaging the North Pacific ecosystem'. In addition the Aleut heritage was further endangered by the flooding of the retail salmon market with cheap farmed fish, effectively putting the Alaskan tribe out of business. The Aleut did not take this lying down however and produced counter evidence that salmon fishing was central to their birthright. According to a report in *The Times* (March 2005), the Aleut produced a mass of archaeological evidence at an Alaska Board of Fisheries meeting, which refuted environmentalists claims that they were damaging the ecosystem. By proving irrefutably that the tribe had been salmon harvesting for thousands of years with no noticeable effect on the environment, the Fisheries Board relented and even extended the salmon season, thereby allowing Aleut ancient traditions to continue.

FISHY FIGURES

110

Weight, in pounds, of the third-placed world record Nile perch caught on Lake Nasser in 2002. First place was 179 pounds and second 120 pounds

THE FISHER AND THE SONG

We Gotta Get Out Of This Plaice, The Animals
Every ling I Do I Do For You, Bryan Adams
Day Bream Believer, The Monkeys
What If Cod Was One Of Us, Joan Osbourne
Almost Pike Being In Love, Nat King Cole
Hake On Me, Aha

WHEN WHAT YOU SAY IS NOT NECESSARILY WHAT YOU MEAN

While anglers love to talk when they're out fishing, their conversations may not be quite as innocent as they seem. Here are a few examples of some hidden meanings:

'Caught anything yet mate?' said with deflated demeanour.
Really means: 'I've had a beast of a day and I want you to have had the same so I don't feel so bad.'

'Caught anything yet, mate?' said with perky conviction.
Really means: 'I've caught loads today and I hope you haven't so I can look superior.'

'Do you mind if I fish here?'
Really means: 'Stop hogging all the action'.

'Saw a lot of fish rising in the next bay.'
Really means: 'Don't want your company just now, mate'.

'Old Fred caught 12 today.'
Really means: 'Are you a local? If you don't know Fred, there's not much point in asking you how things are going, because you won't have the home water knowledge.'

'Caught a lot of fish on the [insert name] fly or the [insert name] bait.'
Really means: 'I've caught enough to satisfy my ego; now it's your turn… that's if there's any fish left in the vicinity.'

TIGHT LINES ON THE THAMES

In 2005 a new angling project called 'Tightlines' was launched on London's rambling network of canals. The project, funded by the Environment Agency and operated by the charity Thames21, works towards introducing a range of fishing skills to both young and old, while fostering a wider respect for London's unique waterside environment. Thames21 not only provides the instructors and the essential gear to learn to fish, but also encourages water users to be more environmentally aware to create clean, safe and sustainable waterways for everyone to enjoy. Find out more at www.thames21.org.uk.

DRUNK GOLDFISH WINS REPRIEVE

In the spirit of tequila aficionados putting worms in their favourite drink, a Canadian bar momentarily started a new craze of goldfish shooters. Apparently customers were inspired by the cult TV series *Fear Factor* and fuelled by a surfeit of the hard stuff, decided to swallow the bar's pet goldfishes whole, having first anesthetised them in a shot glass of neat tequila or Jagermeister, a German liqueur. The fashion was short-lived however after the bar received a complaint from the Calgary Humane Society, which claimed cruelty to the fish. The bar was also then told by the city health inspectors to stop selling the novelty drink on the grounds that the fish may not be fit for human consumption, as they had not been inspected first prior to swallowing.

All this meant the goldfish won a reprieve from a last swim in tequila and instead met their maker as a meal for the pub's other piscatorial resident, the pet catfish. A double-edged sword perhaps?

ENGLAND'S CHANGING CHALKSTREAMS

To the non-angler the sweetly clear meandering streams of Hampshire, Wiltshire and Dorset look as if they have been that way for centuries, when in fact the rivers have been having radical overhauls since time immemorial. According to the Wild Trout Trust, since the forteenth century, if not earlier, England's tranquil chalkstreams have been altered to meet the demands of industry, water supplies, war and agriculture. First came the needs of the old water mills for flour production, then in the seventeenth century the chalkstreams were reverted to water meadow systems presumably in the name of agriculture. But the environmental shake-up didn't end there, for in the twentieth century the rivers changed in nature again when they were widened and deepened to act as deterrents to any invading German forces. In addition, the surrounding meadows were drained and replanted to facilitate crop-growing to support the war effort. And to cap it all, in the post war era, river abstraction for water supplies began in earnest, accompanied by a general draining of the landscape in the name of flood prevention. While they cannot hope to fully restore natural fish habitats to what they were, especially rivers that have seen so much change over the centuries, the Wild Trout Trust has done and continues to do some commendable work on chalkstream habitats. Find out more at www.wildtrout.org.

FISHY FIGURES

144

Height, in inches, of the waterfall at Orrin Falls in Invernshire over which a Scottish salmon was thought to have leapt

PURISM

In the nineteenth century, angling purism was the height of dandified fashion. Then, if you described an angler as a purist, it meant he would only use an exquisitely-made dry fly to catch trout in a river and turn his nose firmly up at any other method. Not only that, but he would only cast the fly upstream and at a rising (actively feeding) trout. If fish were rising downstream or feeding below the surface, in which case a wet fly might catch it, tough, purists fished only the 'dray flay' upstream. Legendary nineteenth-century angler FM Halford can be credited for playing a significant part introducing the dry fly to a much wider audience of anglers; however he did not quite anticipate how his followers would zealously interpret his ideas. What for him began as a novel way of attracting trout on chalk-streams, rapidly turned into a society doctrine practised by those who saw themselves as the angling upper classes with their ideals firmly hooked into dogma. Even Halford as the 'Father of dry fly' began to despair at the behaviour of some of his cult followers declaring: 'Although respecting their scruples, this is in my humble opinion, riding the hobby to death'.

Thankfully the cult of purism has evolved into a more flexible approach and today old prejudices are now all but buried.

FISHY PROVERBS

1. There's no plaice like home.
2. A fish in the hand is worth two in the lake.
3. Birds of a feather make flies.
4. A minnow is known by the company it keeps.
5. Make hake while the sun shines

A PIECE OF THE STREAM

*Going fishing in the British Isles is still a relatively
uncomplicated business; however, if the river, reservoir,
lake or loch needs some form of attention there is always
a bundle of red tape to get through. Here are a few
of the bodies who are in some way involved with
our water:*

Department of Environment, Farming and Rural Affairs
(DEFRA)
Environmental Agency England and Wales (EA)
English Nature
Fishing clubs
Local water authorities
Riparian Owners and lessees
Rivers Agency
Scottish Water
Scottish Fisheries Trusts
Scottish Salmon River Boards
Scottish Environmental Protection Agency (SEPA)
Scottish Natural Heritage (SNH)
World Wide Fund for Nature (WWF)

THE ADAPTABLE WAGGLER

You might be forgiven for thinking that in coarse fishing,
one float is very much like any other. After all it's just a
bobbing little rounded stick. Well no, a float is a bit more
than that. By cunningly adapting the float shape, the angler
allows the bait to be presented in many different ways,
thereby attracting lots of fish. 'Straight wagglers' (stick-like
floats) can in a trice be transformed to make 'body
wagglers' called quaintly by such names as 'onions' or
'missiles'. Top fishermen recommend having separate balsa
wood 'bodies' to quickly slip over the straight waggler and
transform it into a multitude of shapely forms.

FLIES WITH INNUENDO

Flying Cs

Believe it or not, the angler who tied this fly had made the body of it with a condom. In order not to offend other fellow angler's delicate sensibilities, he named the finished creation the flying C. It seems the latex material of the condom is particularly good at keeping the shape of the fly and as it wiggles slightly in the water, fish are greatly attracted to it.

KELLY'S EMERGENCY TROUT

The Kelly Kettle is familiar to anglers wanting a brew up on the river or lake. It's basically a fast-boiling water pot shaped rather like a milk churn; all you need is a small fire or primus for heat, and tea will be served within minutes. However, if you are feeling hungry after catching a few trout but are reluctant to leave the water, the Kelly will come to your rescue, for it will double admirably as a cooking pot.

To do justice to the delicious vaguely sweet flesh of a super-fresh trout caught by your own hand, gut and remove the innards and season the cavity with sea salt and a little white pepper. Remove the head and score the sides with a sharp knife to allow juice absorption. Stuff the trout with a glob of butter, some herbs – fresh tarragon and parsley preferably – and wrap tightly in tin foil. Place the package into the Kelly and heat gently for about 10 minutes or so. Remove and decant into whatever serving dish you have with you and garnish with more parsley and slices of lemon. This goes well with a gentle mustard sauce, green salad and minted potatoes, but if you can't bring the whole shebang with you, just eat the trout with your fingers straight from the tin foil. Finally, remember to wash out the kettle well afterwards.

SCOTLAND'S ALL-BUT-FORGOTTEN TWENTIETH-CENTURY FISHING HEROES

R Macdonald Robertson

Robertson did most of his fishing in Scotland in the 1920s and 1930s. He published three books on Scottish angling adventures between 1935 and 1948. His expansive tales of trout fishing derring-do, laced with a peculiar mix of folklore and fact, are eloquently set amongst lonely moors, racing rivers and stormy lochs. Robertson recalls fishing in a different era, a gentler time when it took days rather than hours to travel the length of Scotland. He is best known for his rollicking tale of the *Muckle Troot O'Dulnain* and for posting his catch south on the train, wrapped in cabbage leaves and sewn into a canvas bag. Although his writings are not much in vogue now, they still stand as enlightening and inspirational reads when compared with much of today's techno-obsessed scribblings.

FREQUENCE GRENOUILLE 2005

According to the French e-zine *Sea-River*, Le Reseau des Conservatoires d'Espaces Naturels (the network of French conservation bodies), held a major environmental exhibition in Spring 2005. The aim was apparently to make the public more aware of the indispensibles that sustain the equilibrium of our planet. These included 'les zones humides, les crapauds, les grenouilles et autre tritons' ('the wetlands, the toads, the frogs and other marine creattures'), which presumably included fish. The event featured guided tours, conferences, films and cartoons for children and exhibitions illustrating the work being done to provide rescue havens for endangered species in different regions of France. Why frog frequency is so important is anyone's guess…

FAMOUS LADIES IN FISHING

Dame Diana Rigg

Esteemed British actress who, when not treading the boards, spends as much time as possible wafting a fly rod. Having begun her fishing career literally learning her (fishing) lines on the River Teith in Stirlingshire, she quickly took to engaging in the theatre of streams and remains a staunch fan of British game fishing.

TO MAKE A BOILE

According to the website www.coarse-fisherman.co.uk, the best boilie (bait) recipe to attract big carp is as follows:

Ingredients
250g base mix
250g ultra-mix
6 medium eggs
Colouring
5ml maple syrup
1 tsp boilie sweetener

Recipe
1. Mix the base mix and the ultra-mix together until thoroughly blended.
2. Form a well in the mix and add in the eggs.
3. Add the colouring and flavouring.
4. Add the sweetener and mix thoroughly.
5. Spread some of the mixture (half at a time) on the table and roll into a sausage shape.
6. Cut into small cubes and roll into balls.
7. Place the 'boilies' into a pan of boiling water and boil for 30 seconds, to one minute.
8. Remove from the water and drain on a tea towel til cool.
9. Place boilies in a plastic bag and dispel the air.

NOSING AROUND

It is said that fish are repelled by certain scents, yet attracted by others. Apparently fish exit stage left when they scent sun block, tobacco or insect repellent in the water. This happens quite frequently as anglers often forget to remove such pongs from their fingers before they tie on the fly. However, the opposite is supposed to occur if a women ties on the fly. Salmon are said to be particularly attracted to a woman's scent. But it's not her Chanel No 5 that provides the attraction; it's her pheromones. Female pheromones apparently transfer on to the fly when a woman ties it on to the line, causing an insatiable response in the male fish population. The number of men using this as a feeble excuse when they fail to catch as many fish as the women has never been fully ascertained.

ANGLING PLOYS
THAT DIDN'T CATCH ON

Professor Peterson's floating chair

The Shetland Museum's photographic archive carries a wonderful picture of a smartly clad angler, complete with what vaguely resembles a pith helmet, fishing in a loch while perched atop a floating chair. The chair legs have been extended fore and aft to accommodate large plastic floats, which appear to be enormous empty jerry cans laid flat on the water surface. Professor Jack Peterson was an avid visitor to the islands in the 1930s. His unusual craft was kept ready for him at the water's edge so he could go afloat as soon as he arrived. However, despite its ingenious design, the traditional Shetland rowing boat won the day and the floating chair sank without trace.

*Cutting across another angler's
drift is not always a good idea*

FLIES WITH INNUENDO

Suspenders

Before you conjure up images of anglers dressed up as if they are about to appear in the *Rocky Horror Show*, this actually refers to a type of fly known as a suspender buzzer. Rather than men clad in fishnet tights the name refers more to the action this small artificial fly makes in the water. A Suspender hangs hook-down, quite literally stuck in the surface film. The fly is tied with a very small bunch of semi-buoyant material at its head, which helps keep it upright in the calm water of the lake. This is to try and imitate a small insect of the *Chironomid* (midge) family and shows the lengths that some anglers will go to get a convincing imitation. Whether the trout register this amount of subtlety, is open to debate.

A FISHING SCRAP

In the nineteenth century, an English angler named Cholmondeley Pennel wrote a book *The Modern Practical Angler*. Pennel was a skilled fisherman, particularly in the art of a wet fly; the black Pennel fly is named after him. However he was none too clever when it came to naming his books. Pennel's tome blatantly copied the title of an already published book *The Practical Angler*, written by that well-respected Scots angler WC Stewart. Not only was the title alike, a good proportion of Pennel's text appeared to be very similar in nature to Stewart's.

Despite protests, the publishers of Pennel's work went ahead and released the book. Immediately, a fierce cross-border war of words erupted. Stewart V Pennel debates followed in that illustrious periodical *The Field* discussing numerous aspects of the two books' similarities. The young Scot flew at Pennel, dander up and hissing that the English angler's book was: 'A compound of plagiarism, absurdity and self deceit'. Pennel spat back his opinions on Stewart's then modern ideas on fishing a fly upstream: 'In spite of Mr Stewart's able advocacy, most anglers have now arrived at the conclusion that fly fishing up stream always or even generally, is a mistake in practice.'

So intense did their arguing become on the pages of *The Field* that the editor eventually had to call a halt. Many years later, Arthur Ransome, editor of the now defunct *Rod and Line Magazine*, admirably summed up their now faintly ridiculous arguments by stating 'They [Stewart and Pennel] have both been long dead and, I suppose fish the Styx, one fishing up and one fishing down and pass each other without speaking'.

THE CORRECTLY DRESSED FLY

In the old days, flies for catching fish were known as 'powerful killers' or 'deadly patterns'; to name a fly with such obvious murderous intent was never considered to be the least bit inappropriate. Nowadays things are different. Here is a fly dressed for our modern, politically correct world:

The politically correct fly

Hook – Biodegradable hand-carved wood not from a rain forest
Tying thread – Cotton from an organically grown crop picked by equal opportunities workers
Body – Unbleached wool from an organically farmed sheep fed on grass grown without pesticides
Wings – Feathers from a corn-fed, free range chicken
Tail – A tuft or two from a bird not on the protected species list

No animals were harmed during the production of this fly

DUBLIN'S NOT SO FAIR

Late in 2004 the Irish Central Fisheries Board had to carry out an emergency rescue of more than 10,000 distressed fish from the Grand Canal Basin in Dublin. An accidental sewage discharge into a section of the waterway caused thousands of fish to go belly up. The Fisheries Board rescuers worked frantically to shift eels, perch, pike and roach to a non-polluted part of the upper canal. Rescue efforts involved giving the gasping fish oxygen via an aerated tank, before transferring them to safer waters. Although many fish did die, the dramatic salvage eventually proved worthwhile, as over 10,000 fish lived to enjoy their new and less polluted home.

ANGLERS YOU MIGHT WANT TO AVOID

Tackle Man

Tackle Man is immediately identifiable by the amount of new and often very expensive fishing equipment dangling about his person. He has hugely inflated expectations of what this tackle can do for his fishing skills. Annoyingly, Tackle Man will often drain you dry of local knowledge and then pass it on to his friends as if he already knew it all. He has little interest in learning about fish species but high interest in having better kit than everyone else. Unless you feel like grovelling for a chance to fish the expensive water that Tackle Man has just leased, he is best to avoid.

SPEAR IT IN

A peculiar form of big game fishing has grown up in antipodean waters. Instead of anglers sitting with a cold beer sunny Caribbean style on plush yachts, anglers have taken to getting in the water with their prospective catch. Their intentions are not benign, however, for they take with them a powerful spear gun. Apparently there are now hotly contested Spearfishing Championships held in Australian and NZ waters. Anglers – or should they be called divers – are allowed only a wet suit, snorkel, mask and a gun equipped with float and line. They must spear the fish and then land it by bringing it to the surface and boating it without the aid of scuba-diving equipment. Target fish species are normally local fish like porae or kahawai but occasionally bigger fish like marlin are landed. In 1997 a marlin of nearly 300 pounds was speared and after an epic tussle was eventually landed. Larger marlin have been taken since. What Hemingway would have thought of this is anyone's guess.

A SMART PARR

If the fry is the baby of the salmon world and the smolt the young immature adult about to migrate to sea to grow, the parr is the pubescent teenager still making his way in river life. Fish breeders will often call them 'precocious parr' meaning they are getting a bit pushy and always trying to carve out their own little niche in the stream. Just like our human teenagers, some fish parr are greedy, inexperienced in life and rather dim in nature. Others show a remarkably well-developed sense of opportunity. These are indeed the precocious ones, nipping in amongst adult salmon in the act of spawning and shedding their own milt on the female eggs. This is perhaps a way of ensuring that if the old male salmon is not up to the job, the young one is there as a backup to produce the goods and continue the species. Nature is nothing if not clever.

HOW FISH GOT THEIR NAMES

Trout

The earliest reference to trout occurs in eleventh-century English literature where trout at that time were called 'sceote' or 'sceotan'. Sceotan seems to be Old English meaning to rush, dart or shoot and obviously describes more the movement of the fish in water, rather than its fishing qualities. After the Normans arrived the sceote name for this fish changed first to 'truht' (Norman French), which then later became trout. By the time Dame Juliana edited the ground breaking *The Treatise of Fishing with an Angle* in 1496, the word trout was firmly established and the Dame enthusiastically describes the trout as 'a ryght feruente byter', literally 'a frequent biter', meaning an excellent sporting fish willing to come to the anglers fly or bait.

TEN MOST INFLUENTIAL FIGURES
IN BRITISH FLY FISHING

All of these anglers have helped to shape British freshwater fishing into what we know today:

Dame Juliana Berners – Fifteenth-century sporting nun and editor of *The Treatise of Fishing with an Angle*, the first fisherman's 'Bible'.

Isaak Walton – Seventeenth-century angler and author of the first edition of the ground breaking *Compleat Angler*.

Charles Cotton – Seventeenth century angler and contributor of skills to the expanded second edition of the *The Compleat Angler*.

Col R Venables – Seventeenth century angler, way ahead of his time recording angling skills which were forgotten, and then reborn in the nineteenth century.

T Stoddart – Nineteenth-century Scottish angler who opened up Scottish angling to the wider view.

WC Stewart – Nineteenth-century Scottish angler who introduced upstream casting with a wet fly.

William Scrope – Nineteenth-century salmon angler who laid down the foundations of the salmon fly and how to fish it.

FM Halford – Nineteenth- and early twentieth-century angler acknowledged as the principal promoter of the art of dry fly fishing in the UK.

GM Skues – Nineteenth- and early twentieth-century angler. The doyen of a style of fishing known as the 'upstream nymph', he introduced new skills to the wider angling public.

Hugh Falkus – Twentieth-century angler who by his writing and broadcasting made game fishing seem much more understandable and therefore accessible.

SILLY NONSENSE FISHING

In the best traditions of the late Stanley Unwin these are
a few appropriate terms relating to fish and fishing:

Giganterums	Fish that get away
Birdsnesters	Kids who constantly get their line in a tangle
Rumticklers	Fish that nibble but do not swallow the bait
Naglers	Fishermen who are always complaining
Smuttiedutters	Trout which are frustratingly rising to tiny impossible-to-imitate insects
Stickleprats	Very small fish that take your bait when you are after bigger fish
Whizzgons	Bait that falls off the hook immediately you cast it out
Numfiddler	Any piece of equipment that is difficult to operate in cold weather

A GREAT ESCAPE

The Hungarian escapologist Harry Houdini was renowned
for extricating himself from strange situations. In the early
1900s a strange 'sea monster' possibly a large whale, was
washed up on a beach at Boston, Massachusetts. This creature was embalmed for public view. Houdini took it upon
himself to be handcuffed and was then forced through an
opening in the side of the monster. The carcass was then
sewn up and sealed with chains. Fifteen minutes later
Houdini escaped and appeared at the monster's side. It is
not known if he sustained his efforts with a little sushi.

A BIT FISHY

What are 'agile darters' and 'laboured swimmers'?
Answer on page 144.

SPARE THE ROD

According to James Leighton Hardy in the book *The House the Hardy Brothers Built*, the illustrous 'House of Hardy' fishing rod manufacturers treated the arrival of fibreglass as a rod-making material in the 1950s, with the deepest of suspicion. They feared rods made of this new material might put their bamboo rods out of business. So much so that they even conspired to make some poor-quality fibre-glass rods in an attempt to convince the public that fibreglass would never catch on and that Hardy's cane rods were still the essential piece of kit.

Their subterfuge failed and fibreglass rods became the new surefire winner from the 1950s to around the mid 1970s, when carbon fibre took over as the new rod material.

A KNOTTY PROBLEM

Odd though it may seem, there is almost a cult surrounding fishermen's knots. Here's a list of just some of the most popular:

Blood knot • Needle knot
Loop to loop • Double grinner
Double turle • Blood bight loop
Trilene knot • Blood loop
Tucked half blood • Double blood knot
Figure of eight • Single grinner
Turle knot • Arbor knot
Safe blood knot • Surgeon's knot

WHAT ANGLERS SUFFER IN
THE NAME OF THEIR SPORT

Limititus

This affliction almost invariably affects reservoir trout fishers. Bag limits are often in force at these fisheries and the angler can become obsessed at making his limit during the allotted time allowed on his day ticket. Quivering wrecks can sometimes be seen towards the day's end thrashing the water to a veritable foam in order to reach the maximum catch limit. Not to do so risks a severely deflated ego and considerable ribbing, if not abject disgrace in the pub afterwards.

MEANEST FISH PREDATORS

Both freshwater and oceanic fish suffer from predation. For example the cormorant eats 25% of its own body weight in fish every day. Predators like the non-native mink or signal crayfish, having been brought to the UK for sources of fur and food respectively, escape or are deliberately released from captivity. Once in the wild they breed quickly and consume huge amounts of small fish fry and fish eggs, which is bad news for fish stocks. Here are 10 of the worst fish-eating culprits:

1. Cormorants
2. Seals
3. Pike
4. American Signal Crayfish
5. Mink
6. Otters (but we forgive them)
7. Zander
8. Mergansers
9. Grass snakes
10. Ospreys (we let them off too)

FISHERS' COMPLAINTS

Anglers are notorious for complaining about the weather; there's always something wrong with it, such as:

It's too bright
It's too cold
It's too hot
It's too wet
It's too dry
It's too windy
It's too still
The water's too high
The water's too low
The water's too clear
The water's too coloured

DIAWL BACH DON'T YOU KNOW

For many years the Welsh fly fishing fraternity rather hid their lights under bushels, and were never as well known in fly tying circles as the English or the Scots. Happily that situation changed for ever in the 1950s when a fly emerged from Wales known as the 'diawl bach'. In Welsh this means 'little devil', an apt name for a pattern that wreaks havoc among trout. This sparse fly, little more than a twist of peacock herl, may have been a long time coming to light, is truly remarkable. Not only is it highly successful in Wales, it also catches trout with almost monotonous regularity across the whole of the UK. Few other patterns can claim to be as consistently productive across the country. Anglers from Loch Leven in Scotland to Blagdon Lake in Somerset swear by these flies, which again and again produce the goods in competition fishing. Today, skilled fly fishers will always have a little devil or two in their fly box.

FISH WARS

Icelandic cod wars

The cold waters around Iceland are rich in fish, particularly cod, a fish that forms the staple ingredient of that beloved British dish, the fish supper. Back in 1958 the Icelanders declared a 12-mile limit around their home shores and excluded other foreign trawlers from fishing there. Britain responded that this rule broke international maritime law and infringed the 'freedom of the seas'. Cod, said the government, would be fished for off Iceland, just as it had always been.

After this announcement feelings ran high. The British Embassy in Reykjavik was stoned and tense scuffles and stand-offs between Icelandic patrols and British frigates became a common occurrence. In 1961 the conflict was resolved, only to start up again in the early 1970s when Iceland pushed out the limit first to 50 miles then 200 miles. More tetchy quarrels resulted at sea until the Brits finally and somewhat reluctantly agreed to annual catches and conservation areas.

FISHY METAPHORS

1. To be in a pretty kettle of fish
2. To have a fish face
3. To be better than a slap in the face with a dead fish
4. To be a cold fish
5. To smell like a fish
6. To have something fishy going on
7. To be told there are bigger fishes in the sea
8. To find he's/she's but a small fish to fry
9. To fish for compliments
10. To flounder around
11. To drink like a fish

Not quite a mermaid but...

LIES, DAMNED LIES AND STATISTICS

In the USA, 16% or 34 million American anglers over the age of 15 went fishing in 2001 and spent over 36 billion dollars on the sport, according to a US National Survey.

To explain the meaning of the saying 'a red herring' is not quite as easy as one might imagine. Back in the eighteenth century the herring could indeed be red, but it did not come fresh from the sea like that. It seems that newly-caught silvery herrings had the alarming habit of going off extremely quickly. In order to preserve the catch a combination of methods could be used, all of which involved a degree of salting and smoking. Different herring ports developed different recipes for the preserving process; for example, Yarmouth had its 'bloater', while Arbroath had its 'kipper' or 'smokie'. Further afield the Germans developed the 'buckling', a rather similar process to the bloater. However the oldest and most famous preserved fish was the 'red herring', which, after lashings of smoking and salting over perhaps two days, did indeed come out a brownish-red.

Nowadays, according to EU regulations, the salt content and carcinogenic qualities of the old red herrings alone might make them impossible to sell; however, the name still lives on albeit under a different guise. Today if we say something is a red herring it means a devious point has been thrown into the argument in order to mislead us. According to *Brewer's Dictionary*, this term is derived from the practice of trailing a (very smelly) red herring across – or more likely around – a field in order to put hunting dogs off the scent of a real fox. Apparently, farmers dismayed at hunters charging through their valuable crops in pursuit of a fox sometimes laid false scents (presumably away from their crops) in order to stop the hounds and huntsmen in their tracks.

The story does not end there, however, for in a typically odd twist, eighteenth-century books on methods of fox hunting do not make any mention of using fish to distract the hounds. In fact in Cox's *Gentlemen's Recreations* circa 1686, a red herring is mentioned as helping to train dogs to follow scent, not put them off it. Cox relates the trailing of a dead fox, cat or in case of necessity a red herring over three or four miles and then 'laying the dogs on the scent'. How the red herring was then converted to a spurious distraction seems never to be properly explained, but then that's red herrings for you.

CASTING A LINE

If you thought fly fishing was simply standing up and waving a stick with a line attached, think again. These are just some of the types of fly line available today:

Double taper • Fast sink • Floating
Ghost tip • Hi Vis (high visibility)
Intermediate • Multi tips • Sink tip • Sinking
Shooting head • Spey lines • Slow sink
Twin-lines • Weight forward •Wetcel's

TERRIBLE FISHING JOKES

It was a boiling hot day on the local river. An old man stood fishing from the bank looking weary and disconsolate. A young fellow angler passing stopped and asked: 'Any luck?' The old man just heaved a heavy sigh. 'Why don't you take a break and come to the pub with me and we'll have a beer,' the young man offered. They made their way to the nearby hostelry and the younger angler bought the old man a foaming pint of ice cold ale.

'Tell me,' he said, 'have you caught anything today at all?'

The old man turned to him and gave a wry grin. 'You're the fourth,' he said.

PHISHING PIRANHAS

In the twenty-first century a new and distinctly nasty form of fishing has appeared. The intention of phishing (the deliberately misspelled name was coined by a computer hacker in the 1990s) is to strip bank accounts clean by using various forms of internet scams. The phisher sends out falsified email requests by banks and other institutions to any computer owner, telling them they must update their customer details. If the unsuspecting prey is caught out by these requests and enters his or her credit card or bank account details, the phisher moves in like the piranha and strips their account down to its bare bones in seconds. If you get request from a phishing piranha, you should throw it back into the cybersea by pressing the delete button.

FIRST STEPS IN FISHING

According to the syllabus of the *Scottish Angling Coaching Course (Level 1)* course participants should have knowledge of:

1. Basic health and safety issues
2. Watercraft
3. Overhead casting
4. Roll casting
5. Entomology
6. Fish biology
7. Knot tying
8. The equipment required and where and when it should be used

The course is designed to give training on how to convey the above skills to novice anglers. Sadly, the bit about participants needing a sense of humour is not on the list.

ONE OF A KIND

The famous River Tweed is unique in several respects:

1. It is the only river in the UK to rise in Scotland, near Moffat, but reach the sea in England at Berwick on Tweed.
2. It is the only river in Scotland to have unique fishing legislation relating solely to its waters.
3. It's also the only river in Scotland that has a statute declaring the care of all fish within the river system, including trout and grayling and not just the more lucrative salmon.
4. It's the only river in Europe where the trout have a 20% salmon gene, which means they have behavioural characteristics more like salmon than trout.
5. The Tweed is the only river in the UK that has 'commissioners' who look after the conservation and general management of the stream.

REEL IT IN

The earliest reports of using a reel when out fishing come from the early seventeenth century. Prior to that time the fishing line (usually made of horsehair) was simply tied on to the end of the rod. The first reels were terribly basic affairs also known as winders and winches. In Scotland a reel was known as a 'pirn'. In game fishing, reels were first introduced to assist the catching of salmon. Some method of storing and controlling the running line during the playing of a large thrashing fish was deemed essential and the reel was born. By the end of the nineteenth century most freshwater anglers were using reels made of brass or wood. From then until now the phrases 'reel it in' or 'wind it in' took over from 'haul it in' which referred more to pulling up a net than applying the rod.

TERRIBLE FISHING JOKES

Q. Why are fish so smart?
A. Because they swim in schools!

FISHING ON THE TELLY

Despite the huge popularity of fishing (there are at least three million regular anglers in the UK), dedicated fishing programmes are mainly confined to satellite TV. This list features some of the current and some of the oft repeated:

Angling Times TV
Bueno Vista
Day Ticket
Fishing on the Edge
Go Fishing
Great Rod Race
Hooked on Fishing
Irish Pike on the Fly
Jungle Hooks
Main Stream
A Passion for Angling
Predators
Rex Hunt's Fishing Adventures
Screaming Reels
Total Fishing

WHAT THE FLOAT DOES

- Shows you when a fish bites
- Helps you cast further
- Holds the bait in the swim
- Helps control of the line
- Sometimes attracts fish to the bait
- Helps you land a fish by guiding it away from weed
- Helps you fish in the dark when it has a lighted top

THE END OF THE KING

The kelt is the end of the line for a male Atlantic salmon. Having survived the rigours of growing up in a British river, migrated to sea, travelled thousands of miles to deep water feeding grounds off Greenland, fed and grown there, returned to its natal river and outlasted all the mean predators along the way, the kelt has spawned with a female salmon and is pretty much on its last legs as it slowly drops back to sea. During this time his condition has been transformed from a spanking athletic bright silver bar to a pathetic-looking creature with flaccid flesh, dull colour and a sad, gaunt scraggy appearance. Many, if not most of these male fish do not make it back to the sea and collapse and die in the river, a sad end to a proud magnificent fish. The remainder that begin to recover in freshwater take on a silvery appearance and from a distance look like fresh-run fish. Anglers catching these fish should by law gently return them with the respect such an extraordinary fish deserves.

FOODY FLIES

Eels

Europeans have consumed freshwater eels for centuries, but the particular type of eel that the fly fisher likes to imitate is the saltwater sand eel. These little eels, only about two or three inches long, form the staple diet of the sea trout as well as other oceanic fish. Despite over-exploitation of eels, mainly by Danish trawlers who scoop them up by the tonne, they are still found in secluded sandy estuaries around the British coastline. Anglers fashion the sand eel fly from glittery fibres, tinsel and shiny paint and they mainly come in olive green, light blue and silver and are a remarkably good imitation of the real sand eel.

BETTER BAITS

A Rubby Dubby Cocktail – This is a particularly ghastly bait used in sea fishing. It is not impaled on a hook but is scattered over the side of the boat in order to attract predatory fish into the vicinity. The best Rubby Dubby should be as fresh and as bloody as possible. Use the heads and entrails of newly killed fish like mackerel and mix together in a bucket, then stir well. Though it may attract stubborn resistance, for best results keep the prepared bait cool in the fridge to lessen coagulation. Preparation of Rubby Dubby is not recommended on the morning after a heavy night out.

Extra Warm Extra Wriggly – Freshwater fish can play very hard to get, especially in chilly weather. A maggot or two on the hook of the fly or just on a bare hook can sometimes work wonders. When the conditions are cold, to make the maggots extra-attractive put a few of them in your mouth for a short period to warm them up. This makes them extra-wriggly, which fish find exciting. Avoiding swallowing may be sensible.

Bed inspections – Oceanic fish love rag worm particularly king rag, but the bait needs lots of TLC to stay in good condition. Pick out any damaged bodies from your freshly dug-up rags, wrap them in newspaper and inspect frequently for signs of a squidgy damp mess. Change the bed daily until all excess moisture is absorbed. This keeps your king rags happy for weeks, lucky them.

FISHY FIGURES

130

Typical length, in centimetres, of the largest
pikes caught in the UK

ANGLING PLOYS
THAT DIDN'T CATCH ON

Needle-eyed hooks

In the late nineteenth century, the making of fishhooks reached new heights of design with 'up eyes' and 'down eyes' being crafted on to the (blunt) end of the hook to enable anglers to tie hook to line securely. Needle-eyed hooks with an eye cut through the end of the hook shank like a needle were made for a time, but anglers quickly gave up on them due to their excessive awkwardness.

FISHY BRITISH PLACE NAMES

1. Shadwell, London
2. Eel Pie Island
3. Laxford Bridge
4. Fishponds, Bristol
5. Ely
6. Loch Nam Breac

PURE PISCES

According to the website www.astroagency.com a person born under the star sign Pisces likes the element of water, exhibits changeable qualities, has negative polarity, is careless and secretive but can be friendly and receptive at the same time. Pisceans generally show a bit of a split personality, sometimes outgoing to the point of recklessness yet on other occasions they remain quietly introverted. Their 'keywords' are sensitivity, sympathy, inspiration and flight. Apparently there is a deep-rooted nature in Pisceans to flee any scene they find a bit uncomfortable – in other words they appear easily spooked. A bit like fish then…

'Scuse me Sir but can I have a bigger rod?'

CROSS-DRESSING CUTTLEFISH

Apparently there are four male giant Australian cuttlefish to every one of the female of the species. This means the male fish have to resort to some subterfuge in order to attract a mate. This they do by disguising their male characteristics and changing their colour in order to resemble the female's mottled appearance. The already paired resident female and male cuttlefish are tricked into believing it's just another lady in their midst. Sneakily when the resident male has its back turned the incoming cross-dresser dashes in and mates with the female. Who said fish are dumb!

HORSES FOR COURSES

The delicate seahorse is one strange fish. If you look at one closely, you'll see that its strange shape is actually that of a deformed fish, made that way by thousands of years of evolution. Its tail alone is a clever piece of work. No other fish in the ocean has a prehensile tail, which acts as an arm to hold them steady in the current; squid and cuttlefish have tentacles, but these are not the same. But the really special thing about the seahorse is the fact that the males give birth and not the females. The male carries and incubates the eggs, which the female deposits in his abdominal pouch, for about six weeks and then goes into labour. Two hundred baby sea horses later he's finished, while the female is nowhere to be seen. How smart is that...

SCRUMPTIOUS BASS

Sea bass are now recognised as one of the UK's best eating fish. The fish command a high price around the country and are the height of gourmet fashion. Sea anglers lucky enough to catch one should bear in mind they can only take it home if it's over 41 centimetres long. They must also remember that there are special designated Bass Nursery Protection Areas (34) off the UK coast and fishing by boat there, for bass, is not allowed.

Once you've landed your legal catch, take it home with pride, gut carefully, for the spines are hypodermics, and season the gut cavity with salt and a little white pepper. Score the thick skin and rub in some garlic and parsley butter. Grill gently until the flesh whitens. Eat with relish and a morsel of samphire if you have it near; if not, a little rocket salad and new minted potatoes does the trick. Top off with a good pinot grigio.

FISH-LIKE SNAKES

*The most primitive types of fish are those
that resemble snakes. These include:*

The lamprey – With an appearance only a mother could love, this eel-like creature has a mouth like a funnel ringed inside with knife-like teeth. Its main aim in life is to suck the lifeblood from its other unsuspecting fishy brethren. Sea and river lampreys are wretched parasites, particularly of salmon; the smaller brook lamprey does not do quite as much damage. Happily the tables have turned on this big sucker, as it is now a popular means of baiting the hook for other predatory species like pike.

The freshwater eel – Eels' most unusual feature is an ability to travel huge distances by water and by wriggling overland. No other fish has this unique ability to swim on land and sea. Not only that, but every eel migrates all the way to the Sargasso Sea to spawn every year. They are common across all of Britain and most of Europe and have been highly prized as a food source.

The garfish – A sea-dwelling species which, from a distance, looks like a two-foot-long green snake with a pronounced thin snout. The fish uses this beak like a truncheon to knock out its prey before swallowing them.

The oarfish – Growing up to four metres long, the oarfish is the longest bony fish in the sea. These are probably the creatures responsible for the sea serpent legends perpetuated by ancient mariners. Despite its fearsome appearance the oarfish is a harmless creature feeding mainly on a diet of plankton. They are very occasionally pulled up by some shocked and surprised anglers off the British coastline, but this is a rare occurrence.

FISH ARE SUPERIOR BEINGS

According to a recent issue of the periodical *Fish & Fisheries*, fish are 'steeped in social intelligence, pursue Machiavellian strategies of manipulation, punishment and reconciliation... exhibit stable cultural traditions and co-operate to inspect predators and catch food'. While this is comforting to know, the Irish have been au fait with the 'fish are smart' concept for years. In Irish mythology, Fionn MacCumhaill was bestowed with superhuman powers when he caught and ate salmon. This fish was called the 'salmon of knowledge'. Nothing new in the sea then.

MOST IRRITATING EVENTS
DURING FISHING EXPEDITIONS

1. You lose the fish of a lifetime, in front of an audience comprising town drunks and small boys.
2. You try to reach a little further and snag your cast in a tree either in front or behind.
3. You walk for miles to reach the remotest water of your dreams only to find you have forgotten the reel.
4. You shut the rod in the car door before or after going fishing (before is worse).
5. You jump in the car and drive off, straight over the reel or the rod or both.
6. You drive home with the rod sticking out of the window, the line catches in a tree and whizzes out behind you leaving a lengthy and expensive trail of knitting.

FISHY FIGURES

72

Number of locations in England where the zander has been found

SALMON IN A BASKET

One of the first methods used to catch a salmon was not by rod and line but by using a wicker basket. This would be placed in the river below a waterfall. Salmon running up the river would try and leap the falls and those that were not successful fell back into the waiting basket below. At one time at the falls of Arkaig, near the country estate house of Achnacarry, the resident cook had an ingenious early warning rope system installed. If a salmon landed in the basket, the weight of the fish pulled on the rope, which activated a bell in the kitchen. Cook would then know that salmon was going to be the main dish that evening.

A BIT FISHY

What was the 'carshalton dodge'?
Answer on page 144.

TO SKIN A FISH

Recent developments in tanning procedures have meant that once discarded fish skins from species like salmon, stingray, shark or cod are being recycled and made into fish leather products. Manufacturers are now able to produce a range of fish skin apparel and accessories which are said to match the durability of crocodile leather, while having a similar softness and texture to manmade fibres. Houses like Dior have experimented with pink salmon shoes, Bottega Veneta retailed stingray clutch bags for over a thousand dollars and salmon bikinis have been marketed by Skini, the Scottish fashion house. Ireland, France, Canada, USA and New Zealand have already got in on the recycling act and manufacturers are hoping to hook up with plenty of new customers.

ANGLING MAGAZINES
PAST AND PRESENT

Prior to the days of the internet, fishing magazines thrived. The following list includes some live publications and and a few of the casualties.

Fish for the live ones!

American Angler
American Fly Fisher
Anglers Mail
Angling Times
Coarse Fisherman
Field & Stream
Fly Fishing & Fly Tying
Improve your Coarse Fishing
Sea Angler
Trout Fisherman
Trout & Salmon
Countrysport
Fishing Gazette
Game Gazette
Rod and Line
Salmon Trout & Sea Trout
Scottish Angler
Strike!
Total Fly Fisher
Waterlog

LIES, DAMNED LIES AND STATISTICS

In Britain in 2006 more that 4 million people went fishing, according to the UK Environment Agency. That's 7% of the population with an angling interest. It figures that more and more people are getting hooked.

FOODY FLIES

Squid

Forget the chewy calamari so beloved of most Spanish restaurants, these flies are made to look like a small but very colourful swimming squid. The flies are used almost exclusively in saltwater fly fishing where 'squids' come in purple, pearl or chartreuse hue. With their impressionistic trailing tentacles made of fine nylon fibres combined with tinsel, beady eyes and longish shiny head, they are said to be very attractive to sea-dwelling fish like barracuda or tarpon, especially if the angler fishes them on a pulsing retrieve, just like the real thing.

VIRTUALLY CAUGHT

The 2005 Miami Boat Show featured a fishing competition sponsored by such diverse organisations as the International Bill Fish Network, Scopinich Fighting Chairs and the American Fisheries Society. Nothing unusual in that you might think; except that the competition took place indoors, there was no sea spray, no fish were really caught and no blood was shed. Despite this odd setting, competitors still won angling accolades, for what they were participating in is a novel sport known as virtual big game fishing. Anglers have just less than two and a half minutes to try and land a monster cyber sailfish. The competitors are strapped into a fighting chair, given a digitally controlled fishing rod and reel and watch a film on a sceen in front of them. The clever part is the weight on the line they have to wind in, which acts in time with the leaping sailfish on the screen. Apparently the participant gets a great workout without ever coming into contact with the real thing. And it's good for fish conservation, too.

WHAT'S WILD?

Anglers speak about wild trout in tones of deep reverence. Normally they are referring to trout that have procreated naturally in a wild setting. These trout must be distinguished, however, from 'native' fish, which are the original colonisers from the last Ice Age. Because of the amount of stocking of trout (grown in hatchery tanks) into waters containing native fish, a practice begun in Victorian times and still going on today, many ancient gene lines have been corrupted. Thus many rivers and lakes that are described as containing wild trout actually contain fish of extremely mixed bloodlines, while native trout waters contain the pure non-genetically modified versions. These fragile fish populations (mainly occurring in Scotland) are the ones that need to be carefully conserved, for they are at the centre of our angling heritage.

The late, gravel-voiced George Melly admitted to having been so excited about catching a wild trout he had to dash into the bushes and masturbate with a dock leaf. Who knows what he would have done if he'd hooked a native...

STICK AN OAR IN

In 2004 a woman angler busy fishing for cod with squid bait off the Cleveland coast of north east England caught and landed a scarce monster of the deep; an oarfish weighing 63.5 kilogrammes and measuring 3.5 metres long. Unfortunately scientists were left bitterly disappointed as, before they could get there and, perhaps not realising the rarity of the catch, the woman sliced it up and put it in her freezer. Sadly, oarfish are plankton feeders and are flavourless fish. They do not make good eating. It is not known if the household are still munching through the oarfish.

THE ONES THAT GOT AWAY

Some fish are territorially beyond the reach of even the most determined fishermen. Those that dwell in the dark canyons of the deepest ocean beds are almost impossible to catch, and the specimens that have been rounded up by submarines have often exploded with the pressure change. Here are a few of them, and their freakish physical attributes:

Bristlefish
(Long and snakelike, with a line of glowing
dots on its underside)

Deep sea angler fish
(Similar to shallower-dwelling species, but
with much nastier teeth)

Black swallower
(Distensible stomach that can become
bigger than the rest of its body)

Stoplight loosejaw
(The only creature in the world with
a flashing red light on its head)

THE IDEAL ANGLER SHOULD...

1. Be magnanimous; accept that failure is quite common.
2. Realise that angling is a lifelong learning experience to be savoured and worked on.
3. Learn from their mistakes.
4. Share accumulated knowledge and experiences with others, especially youngsters who are the life blood of the sport. You will get back more than you give out.
5. Get involved and be informed in matters of fish conservation, both in the practical and the scientific.
6. Treat fishing as a big adventure not an endurance test.

FAMOUS LADIES IN FISHING

Dame Juliana Berners

Dame Juliana was the principal (and the best known) editor of the very first British fishing book *The Treatise of Fishing with an Angle*, published in 1496. An educated, devout but sport-loving nun, she helped to bring together previously amassed fishing knowledge, both from European and British quarters. Though she is sometimes wrongly recorded as the sole author, the Dame must nevertheless be given huge credit in the assembling of this milestone work, which, 500 years on, remains at the pinnacle of fishing literature.

SPINNING AROUND

When anglers talk about spinning or spinners, they could be talking about either of two things. On the one hand spinners can be those fishy shapes made of shiny metal with a mean looking treble hook on the end. You will see anglers using short rods to whiz their spinner out attached to clear monofilament line. Having cast out, it's just a question of reeling it back in furiously while hoping an unsuspecting fish will snap up the spinner either in a fit of pique or because they think it's a rapidly escaping prey. This simple ploy is known as spinning. But the other kind of spinner is of a much more delicate nature. Spinners in fly fishing are the filmy adult version of an up-winged fly like a Blue Winged or Large Dark Olive. Fly fishers revere these flies and make imitations of spinners as trout love them. Quite how the insect got its name is unclear but it seems to be something to do with the behaviour of the fluttery dancing clouds of these insects, often seen busily 'spinning' above river pools on warm evenings.

WHAT ANGLERS SUFFER IN
THE NAME OF THEIR SPORT

Angler's Cramp

Angler's Cramp usually occurs after the preparatory stages of the day's activities, when all the lines have been tied, the flies fixed and the bait hooked. The condition strikes when the angler attempts to hurl his line into the water to find his casting arm firmly stuck behind his back. If the freeze extends to the angler's hand locking the rod at an awkward angle, it can be quite difficult to fit the patient into an ambulance, and firemen with cutting tools should be on hand to section the rod. Cod liver oil can help too.

A BIT FISHY

Which is the odd one out?
Ale wife, may fish, chad, houting, King of the Herring.
Answer on page 144.

NELSON THE ANGLER

Not only was Admiral Nelson a legendary seafaring hero, but also he was apparently very skilled in wielding the fly rod. He spent most of his angling time upon the River Wandle, a famous chalkstream in his day but now sadly in need of restoration. Legend has it that he fished the river on the morning of the day he left to join his ship the Victory on 13 September 1805. Appropriately in 2005, the two-hundredth anniversary of Nelson's death, the Salmon and Trout Association launched fundraising efforts to help revive the fortunes of the River Wandle. Fundraising dinners were organised and all proceeds were put towards the Jet Set Club headed by Dr David Bellamy, which promotes the River Wandle Restoration Project.

OLD PISCATORIALS – NEW EDITORIALS

Catch of the day

FAMOUS ANGLERS AND THEIR DAY JOBS

Ian Botham – *Retired cricketer*
Bernard Cribbens – *Actor*
Nick Faldo – *Golfer*
Sir Max Hastings – *Former editor of the* Daily Telegraph

THE GILLIE'S REVENGE

The gillie (a Scottish term meaning young boy and/or helper) will act as a guide to the salmon fisher on a river. He can quite literally make or break the day. Gillies are known for their deep abiding love, not only of fishing but also of whisky. Should their charge fail to regularly produce a surfeit of the latter, gillies have been known to extract revenge by the following means:

1. Fail to tell the guest his fly was cracked off on a stone behind at least half an hour ago, and leave him thrashing away with a long piece of nylon and no chance of hooking anything.
2. Give the myopic guest a casting stance on a flat stone covered in a thin layer of slippery algae and then tell him to cast vigorously.
3. Turn the boat into the wind and gun the engine hard while the guest is still trying to don his waterproof.
4. Put his charge on a river pool with a surfeit of undergrowth and point out the best salmon lies happen to be with gorse bushes in front and leafy alder trees directly behind.

GOLDFISH STRIKES IT LUCKY

Following floods engulfing Carlisle in January 2005, two goldfish were rescued from the local football ground as water was being pumped from the pitch. One of the fish was recognised as 'Judy', a local pet who had been carried away in the floods. Judy's owner has agreed the fish can be adopted as club mascot for the Carlisle United team. The lucky goldfish will be cared for by the daughter of the club owner who had pluckily saved the fish from being hoovered back up in the floodwater. When Judy is not on mascot duty the second fish will act as substitute.

LIES, DAMNED LIES AND STATISTICS

A report by the Environment Agency in 2006 stated that 2.6 million of the 43 million people over 12 in England and Wales went fishing in freshwaters in the last year.

CORACLES

The coracle is a really devilish form of water transportation. One false move and it tips you in the drink. Nevertheless the Welsh have persevered with this small personal boat for many centuries. The coracle has a rounded wooden frame covered with an animal skin and looks rather like an upturned turtle shell. The fisherman sits on one single seat in the interior and propels himself along with a very basic oar, little more than a plank of wood. Rod fishing is not much done from the coracle as they are extremely light and unstable craft and any enthusiastic casting is more likely to see you swimming; instead, fishermen have traditionally strung a net between two coracles and hauled in the fish in this way. Fishers take their coracle to the river by carrying it on their back. They are easily recognised as they look like a large beetle walking on two legs.

TERRIBLE FISHING JOKES

A man knocks on the door of a house and says to the woman who opens it: 'Good afternoon, I'm looking for Mr Jones.'

'I'm Mrs Jones,' says the woman. 'Can I help?'

'Oh no,' says the man, 'it's Fishing Club business; can you tell me where I can find him?'

The woman replies: 'Well in that case, go down to the river and look for a stick with a worm at both ends.'

A TALE OF VOE

Shetland is not perhaps the first place you would think of as a famous fishing destination. A trip to the Hampshire chalk-streams maybe, but a long troop involving rough sea crossings and overnighters all the way to Shetland?

What on earth for? But although Shetland is more or less forgotten now as a fishing destination, early twentieth-century anglers went there in droves. Their quarry was the large sea trout, which were then prolific along Shetland's indented coastline. Although saltwater fishing on the islands never quite achieved the cult status of 1930s big game tunny fishing off Scarborough, a considerable number of the great and good braved the long trip to these islands. Not for nothing did northern men of the cloth hold group meetings on Shetland during July and August, the peak times for sea trout fishing. Local legend has it that they

would time their devotions so that they could stop and high-tail it down to the shore to fish for the big trout coming in on the turn of the tide.

Anglers fished predomi-nantly in sea 'voes', a word that comes from ancient Norse meaning a firth, bay or creek. The fishers would position themselves in these long rocky inlets so that the fish would have to pass them by as they headed up on the incoming tide toward the freshwater river at the head of the voe. The sea trout ran up and spawned in these fresh-water burns in October, but for the rest of the year they would mooch around the Shetland coastline, feeding on the rich diet of crustaceans and sand eels. Thus the incoming tide would bring a shoal of sea trout into the voe and angling timing was critical. The fish did not stay long, just long enough to nose the waters of their natal stream before scooting seaward again, so it was up to the angler to be in the right place at just the right time.

Sadly the sea trout fishing reached a nadir in the late 1960s, when for some inexplicable reason the numbers of sea trout started to fall and, unsurprisingly, the number of wealthy anglers coming to Shetland dropped off. Come the 1980s and the advent of fish farming, the wild sea trout numbers further declined and today Shetland fly fishers have largely left the voes to concentrate on the islands excellent freshwater lochs. Which is another little piece of British angling history gone west.

BIRDS OF A FEATHER

Ever since the first angler devised the first artificial fly, feathers have been an essential ingredient in their make up. These are just some of the birds that have supplied their plumage:

Blackbird
Cockerel
Mallard
Grouse
Hen
Peacock
Pheasant
Sea Gull
Starling
Teal

MATERIALS THAT HAVE BEEN USED TO MAKE FISHING RODS

Ash • Bamboo cane • Blackthorn • Carbon Fibre
Crab tree • Fibre Glass • Greenheart • Hazel • Hickory
Lancewood • Whalebone • Willow • Yew

FAMOUS GAME FISHING VENUES
AROUND THE UK

Across Britain there are fisheries with long-established and well-deserved reputations. These are a few of the best known:

In England	In Ireland
River Test	Lough Corrib
River Itchen	Lough Melvin
Blagdon Lake	Loch Erne
Chew Reservoir	Lough Conn
Rutland Reservoir	Lough Mask
Bewl Reservoir	Foyle Fishery
River Wharfe	Burishoole Fishery
River Teviot	Delphi Fishery

In Scotland	In Wales
River Tweed	River Towy
River Spey	River Teifi
River Tay	River Nevern
River Dee	Llyn Brenig
River Don	Talyllyn
Loch Leven	Lake Vyrnwy
Loch Watten	
Lake of Menteith	

FAMOUS LADIES IN FISHING

Muriel Constance Foster

The little diary *Days on Sea Loch and River* written and illustrated by Muriel Foster, stands as testimony to angling from another, more genteel, time. Muriel's superb watercolour drawings (she studied at the Slade School of Art) bring life to her meticulous handwritten recording of fishy successes and failures and the wonderful asides like 'Weather altogether beastly', make for unique reading.

MAIN CAUSES OF DEGRADATION OF FRESHWATER FISH HABITAT

1. Abstraction of water for human consumption
2. Livestock grazing and incursion into water courses
3. Afforestation in areas where fish would normally spawn
4. Agricultural practices particularly drainage ditching
5. Industrial effluent discharges
6. Road workings adjacent to the watercourse
7. Sewage discharge near estuarine habitats

A BIT FISHY

Who were the Rebeccaites?
Answer on page 144.

WHAT SALMON – AGAIN!

Legend has it that in the seventeenth and eighteenth centuries the indentures of apprentices contained a clause stating that salmon was not to be served to them on more than two or three occasions per week. While this was a lovely tale, it was subsequently proven that no such exact clause existed. In 1955 a Mr Cohen wrote a paper called Apprentices and Salmon in the *Transactions of the* *Woolhope Naturalists Field Club Hertfordshire* (Vol XXXV, part 1), which discovered that poorly paid farm workers insisted on a diet of salmon being limited to just a few days per week, but dispelled the myth of the apprentice indenture clause.

Whatever the truth, it just goes to show how prolific salmon were in British rivers in the past. It is now on the Protected Species list.

SUPERSTITIONS OF THE SEAFARERS

Pass the salt

In Scotland, superstition has it that salt must never be mentioned while at sea. To do so was thought to bring immediate bad luck upon the fishing boat and its crew. There is a story from 1905 of an Eyemouth boat which ran short of salt while out trawling. The skipper hailed a Yarmouth drifter with the words: 'We need something we dinna want to speak aboot'. The English skip shouted back 'Is it salt ye want?' to which the Scot replied indeed it was and the precious commodity was handed over without mentioning it by name. The Scottish crew escaped certain doom by keeping below decks out of earshot while the discussion was going on.

SYMBOLIC FISH

Fish drawings, motifs or symbols crop up again and again throughout history, sometimes as decoration, sometimes as meaningful symbols. The Romans adorned their villa walls with ornate drawings of decorative fish while the early Christians adopted the fish more as a religious symbol, which has endured until the present day. The Normans featured fish in their architecture and monuments, while the Anglo Saxons had fish emblazoned on anything from swords to drinking vessels. These fish seem to be decorative, but during the eighth century AD the Picts of northern Scotland erected their Pictish stones and these feature fish symbols the meaning of which is lost in antiquity.

It was not until Dame Juliana Berners's *The Treatise of Fishing with an Angle* was published in 1496, that we see fish and angling connected in an arty drawing on the book's frontispeace. And the rest as they say is history…

BORDER ESK GOES ENGLISH

The fishing rights and ownership of the Border Esk River, which begins its life in Scotland but tips into the sea in England, have long been the cause of a bitter dispute between the two countries – for 550 years, in fact. Epic cross-border spats over salmon fishing have been going on since 1450. It seems that the English built a dam that trapped the salmon in their section of the river, effectively stopping any fish from reaching the Scottish half of the river. This led to endless rows and fights with not a little blood being shed over some 300 years before a rather inadequate compromise was reached which allowed some of the fish to swim upstream. In 2005 the Scottish Executive passed legislation allowing the English to demand a rod licence fee from anglers wanting to fish anywhere on the River Esk in both Scotland and England. Until this time in Scotland no rod licence had been necessary – only a permit fee was paid. This caused some nationalistic anglers with long memories to throw their hands up in horror; they say this is just another example of the English unfairly taking the lion's share. It would seem echoes of the '45 Rebellion loom large, even now…

ALT TOGETHER NOW

In Gaelic, a river or burn in Scotland is usually known as 'alt', which is sometimes corrupted to 'ault'. This prefix is often assimilated into place names. Here's a few:

Altnaharra • Altnabreac • Altandhu
Altnacreig • Altass • Aultbea
Ault a'chruinn • Aultguish
Aultmore • Aultnamain
Aultnagoire • Aultgrishin

FAMOUS LADIES IN FISHING

HM Queen Elizabeth the Queen Mother

The late Queen Mother was a highly skilled salmon fisher, frequently casting flies on Scottish waters including the Thurso near her beloved retreat the Castle of Mey in Caithness and the River Dee at Balmoral. By the time she was in her mid 20s her expertise with a salmon rod was already legendary. After the tragic loss of her husband the King, she found some solace in angling, and few could match her determination to catch fish in all weathers.

OLD PISCATORIALS – NEW EDITORIALS

A gal's best friend is her gillie

FISHY FIGURES

80

Number of chromosomes present in a brown trout

WHAT TO DO WITH THE FISH

Smoke it • Poach it • Pickle it • Salt it • Grill it
Fry it • Bake it • Barbecue it • Steam it • Souse it

SCOTS WA HAE

Tongue-twisting Gaelic names for Scottish lochs usually derive from the waters' distinguishing features. A loch's name can help you decide if it is worth fishing.

Here are a few examples of common loch names:

Loch Clach or **Nan Clach** – A stony loch. Often refers to a boulder-strewn shoreline and might mean difficult wading. Check for other clues as to the nature of the environment, however, as sometimes infertile stony-looking waters hold big fish, especially if they are spring-fed.

Loch Beg – A little loch. A very common loch name in Scotland and only gives an indication of water size rather than fishing quality.

Loch Fada – Means a long loch and it's going to be a long stretch of water to cover.

Loch Mhor or **Lloch More** – A big loch.

Loch na Moine – Loch of the bog, probably with a distinctly difficult squidgy shoreline and dark peaty water. Quality rating doubtful and trout in acidic water tend to remain small throughout their adult lives.

Loch Nam Breac – Breac is the Gaelic word for trout and therefore this loch is likely to hold a reasonable supply.

Loch Meadie or **Loch Caol** – both these names mean a narrow loch where your neighbour on the far shore is always in view.

CHALLENGING FISHING
GEMS ACROSS THE UK

Every angler has some waters he or she would like to keep secret: special places where time is forgotten and the magic of fishing takes over. These recommendations are for the avid game fisher who likes a challenge:

River Frome, *Dorset:* A meandering gin clear chalkstream where golden gleams of big trout are glimpsed between waving ranunculus. Testing, comparatively inexpensive fly fishing for wary trout in beautiful Dorset.

River Nevern, *Pembrokeshire:* Inspiring small spate river where sewin and salmon rush into dark tree lined pools. When the water is fining down after heavy rain this is the place to be in west Wales.

Lough Melvin, *Northern Ireland:* Enigmatic west coast Irish lough full of trout mysteries including the famed Gillaroo and Sonaghen. Difficult enigmatic water at times but a place which once discovered holds you in its spell.

River Tummel, *Perthshire, Scotland:* A demanding tributary of the bigger River Tay where trout, salmon and grayling hide extremely well in clear gravely pools. Bewitching, beguiling and bloody minded all in one go.

Loch Watten, *Caithness Scotland:* This shallow and rich clear water loch just screams wild trout at you. A place to enjoy long drifts in the boat and watch the sun go down.

TERRIBLE FISHING JOKES

Q: Where do fish keep their money?
A: In the river bank.

WHAT ANGLERS SUFFER IN
THE NAME OF THEIR SPORT

Castinear-itus

This is a painful ailment normally associated with the fly fisher. That prize fish always seems just out of reach, and in one superhuman effort the angler will try and launch his line just that little bit further. At precisely the same moment a gust of wind strikes and instead of going that extra yard the fisher hooks his ear and goes the extra mile to outpatients to have the hook of the fly removed under local anaesthetic.

THE FISHER AND THE SONG

Pike A Virgin, Madonna
Take Me Trout, Franz Ferdinand
Big Kipper, Elton John
It's A Fin, Pet Shop Boys

ICEBERG AHOY

Antarctic fishing trawlermen collectively heaved a huge sigh of relief when in 2005 the drift of the world's largest iceberg, christened rather unimaginatively the 'B15-A', finally came to a halt. In late April it crashed into the Drygalski ice tongue with no casualties reported. Apparently this big bang, billed as 'the collision of the century', was supposed to happen some three months earlier. However, during January the icy colossus got stuck aground on a shallow sea mount.

This unexpected delay caused more upset by cutting off shipping routes than the eventual collision itself which was described by the head of the Oceans and Ice Unit as more like a bump in the night than the collision of the century.

FISHING FLIES NAMED AFTER WOMEN

Many flies used in trout or salmon fishing are
named after or appear to be connected with women.
For example, the 'Alexandra fly' is named after Princess
Alexandra. Here are a few more:

1. Kate McLaren
2. Meg in her braws
3. Alexandra
4. Damsel nymph
5. Yellow Sally
6. Baby doll
7. Dogsbody
8. Golden Anna
9. Heather moth
10. Ladybird
11. Merry widow
12. Painted lady

HERON THE HUNTER

The traditional method by which a heron catches its prey is by standing rock-still on one leg, head on one side, stealthily stalking the unsuspecting fish that is quietly minding its own business in the pool below. In a blink of that wickedly beady black eye, the heron shoots its long neck out, seizes the fish in its beak and with a quick toss of the head, the poor fish is dispatched straight down the bird's gullet. According to a recently published survey led by the McGill University in Montreal, herons have 'learned' fly fishing techniques. Birds have apparently been sighted catching flies in their beaks, dropping them like an artificial fly upon the surface of the water and then waiting for a fish to rise to the bait, whereupon the smart heron swallows it whole.

THE SECRET OF THE SHOAL

Going into a vast swirling shoal is the little fish's secret weapon against larger predators. Those underwater films of oceanic fish rising and falling in great columns, circles and twists are not staged for the camera. However hypnotically beautiful the shoals may be, the fish are swimming like that with only one objective in mind – self preservation. Apparently, bigger predators are confused by the brilliant flashing silver clouds initiated by the little darting fish as they switch directions with lightning speed. Interestingly, the fish at the centre of the shoal are not necessarily the safest. Predators befuddled by the flickering fishy lights in front of them tend to bludgeon into the core of the shoal with mouths wide open and it's a swift end for those unlucky enough to be in the middle at the time.

ANGLERS YOU MIGHT WANT TO AVOID

The Local Expert

Local Experts talk incessantly about themselves and their latest successes, engaging you in a weird sort of continuous loop of conversation into which you fail to insert a word. They are easily recognised by their flushed and seriously smug faces when fish have been caught. However, if they have not bagged anything, they instantly vanish so as to avoid the post-match analysis in the pub. Irritatingly their knowledge is often good for their local patch but take heart in the fact that it can fluctuate wildly if they fish unfamiliar territory.

A BIT FISHY

Which is the odd one out?
Truff, sprod, scurf, thorm, mort.
Answer on page 144.

DAMMED IF I DO

Imagine you are a fish for a moment. There you are swimming away quite happily knowing your own limits, where the lake world begins and ends. Suddenly this great whoosh of water comes in and before you know it, there you are feeding in a field! For a while, life is just rosy. All those juicy worms and snails you could never get at before are now right there in front of you. You eat better than you have done in years. But after the feast, the famine arrives. All the extra food disappears, washed away in waves twice as big as they ever were before. And the lake has something weird about it. Your world is not the same. The water goes up and down alarmingly especially when some gigantic gate opens at one end and everything gets sucked out.

Welcome to your new life in the reservoir.

SEA TROUT PIONEERS

Sir Herbert Maxwell

Sea trout fishing has always been an incredibly difficult branch of game angling to get exactly right. This is due as much to the fickle, secretive nature of the fish as it is to the anglers' skill. But Sir Herbert Maxwell, an eminent nineteenth-century scientist, was one of the first to define the techniques necessary for successful sea trout angling, which he outlined in his book *Salmon and Sea Trout*, published in 1898. Maxwell was the first to acknowledge sea trout as a separate species, albeit by misnaming them 'salmon trout'. These fish, he declared, were different from Atlantic salmon and therefore the angler might need to use different techniques to fish for them. Prior to Maxwell's book, the sea trout was not much recognised as anything other than a pest that got in the way of salmon angling.

THE OTTER – FRIEND OR FOE

The otter and the angler have had a strange on-off love affair over the centuries. As far back as 600AD fishermen have used otters to help them catch fish. During the Tang Dynasty, fishermen reared wild otters by hand. The otters were so well trained they would, on command, swim out and drive unsuspecting shoals of fish towards the waiting nets. This practice continued in China until the beginning of the twentieth century. In Europe similar tales are told of otters being trained to 'round up' fish for the fishermen's nets.

Comparable tales of this symbiotic relationship continued in England until around the nineteenth century, when suddenly the otter took on a completely different mantle and became regarded as the angler's foe rather than his friend. Gamekeepers on Victorian sporting estates took to hunting, trapping or shooting otters as they insisted that they were taking too many valuable fish from the rivers. Otter populations dramatically diminished and it was not until the 1950s that otter hunting finally came to a halt. Scientific evidence finally proved that the wild otter fed more on eels in freshwater and crustaceans while at sea. Although they were partial to game fish, they did not do the huge amount of damage that the old gamekeepers had alleged.

While the wild otter has been accepted back into angling circles, there is a peculiar irony in the fact that one of the most lethal devices in fish poaching is called the 'otter'. This is a plank of wood with a string of baited hooks beneath it, which is roped up and then floated out into river or lake and left to bob about while fish impale themselves on the hooks. The poacher then returns, pulls in the rope and the 'otter' obligingly brings in the catch.

ANGLERS YOU MIGHT WANT TO AVOID

The Cagoule

Imagine a processed-cheese sandwich on white bread in human form, and you have the Cagoule. The fishing first-cousin of the civilian 'Anorak', he is often seen huddled on the bank wrapped up in an oversized, crinkly waterproof, clinging onto his rod and wondering what's gone so wrong in his life. As such he has known to wallow there for three days without a break – or a catch. Lacking any serious knowledge of the finer arts of fishing, the Cagoule comes to the river for want of other things to do. His paucity of skill leaves him with no alternative but to channel disen-chantment down the fishing-line, in the hope that the fish will leap out of the water in order to avoid it. Sadly, this only drives them towards other anglers' hooks. Be warned: the Cagoule's voice can trigger off an existential crisis.

A RING OF TRUTH

One of the oddest catches of 2005 has to be a sailfish caught off the coast of Florida with a wedding ring round its nose. Not only that but the angler Eric Bartos who caught it knew just how it got there. Two years previously, he had symbolically slipped it on the fish's beak and returned it to the sea. He did so to symbolise the break up of his marriage, his lost love and the fact that he felt his love for

fishing was at that time stronger. This time Bartos retrieved the wedding ring and gently released the fish back to the water.

Upon returning to shore few would believe this weird coincidence but after taking a lie detector test, Bartos's tale does indeed appear to be true. His story so impressed his ex-wife she contacted him after over two years of silence and told him it might be a sign to 'make peace'.

WHEN THE CANAL WON'T DO

Up until the 1970s, most British anglers were reasonably content to fish their local waters, and only a small minority headed for exotic destinations, with the sole purpose of fishing. Nowadays with increased leisure time, cheaper flights and greater spending power, anglers are venturing further afield. These are just a few of the advertised destinations from which you can now choose:

Alaska • Australia
Bahamas • Baja
Belize • British Columbia
Canada • Christmas Island
Costa Rica • Cuba
Denmark • Egypt
Florida • Greenland • Holland
Iceland • India
Kamchatka • Kenya
Kola Peninsula
Madeira • Mauritius
Mexico • Mongolia
Montana, USA
Namibia • Nepal
Newfoundland • New Zealand
Norway • Patagonia • Peru
Russia • Sardinia
Seychelles • South Africa
Spain • Sweden • Slovenia
Thailand • Venezuala

FISHY FIGURES

111

Value, in millions of US dollars, of the commercial and recreational fisheries on Long Island Sound, USA

THE BOAT THAT I TOW

A humongous 322lb halibut hooked by a sea angler off the Norwegian coast proved too heavy to land in his 30ft boat. Fortunately he had put to sea with an industrial-sized engine, which run at full throttle, enabled the surprised but happy angler to literally tow the live catch back to the harbour. He then netted a tidy sum by selling it to a local fish-processing plant. At least he could tow his catch to land; anglers fishing from light rowing boats without an engine, sometimes find the tables completely turned. In 1998 a large salmon towed a rowing boat and its two occupants around on remote Loch Loyal in Sutherland for over half an hour before the fly eventually came loose and the fish escaped capture. Truly the one that got away.

JUST KEEP SWIMMING

When designing a family or city coat of arms, the herald had often to incorporate a fish in the drawing. This could be done in four different ways. The fish could be 'endowed', swimming to the left (as seen by the viewer) with a distinct arched back. Alternatively, it could be 'hauriant', which meant it was swimming vertically upwards. Failing that it could be 'naiant', which meant it was swimming in a straight line to the left as seen by the viewer or last but not least, the fish could be 'uriant', sometimes spelt 'urinant'. This last term meant swimming or diving vertically downwards.

TERRIBLE FISHING JOKES

Q. What is the fastest fish in the water?
A. A motorpike.

And we have lift off...

ANGLERS YOU WON'T MIND MEETING ON THE RIVERBANK

The Apprentice

Apprentice anglers are furiously keen. They are usually the first to arrive at the water. Normally they have little time for contemplative analysis. The rod will be up in a flash and the water whipped to a foam before you have even drawn breath. If they are very young, this angler may develop a more patient, thoughtful approach; however, should they be in their middle years, conversion to higher ground may be more difficult. Apprentices are given to asking the same question again and again in slightly different ways and then not listening to the answer. They are instantly recognised by ear-splitting grins when things are going well, and slumped shoulders and fat lips when things are not.

Anglers have always preferred to get to exactly where the fish are without the fuss of hiring a boat and carting with them all the paraphernalia that boat fishing attracts (oars, anchor, etc). In 2004 it seemed as if their prayers might have at last been answered. *The New York Times* reported that Yoav Rosen from Massachusetts had been granted a patent under the name 'Upright human floatation apparatus and propulsion mechanism' for an invention that allowed him to walk upright on water. Over 100 patents have been granted for water-walking apparatus in the last 150 years, but none of them has worked. Mr Rosen said that he had been working on the idea since he was 11 years old and had worked single-mindedly on various prototypes before coming up with what he saw as a winner.

Inspired by DaVinci's ideas for water walking which, according to models in the Leonardo Museum, look like a skier with two large floats on his feet using poles to keep him upright, Rosen had a similar but novel design. Gone are the ski poles, and the pontoons on the feet have flaps attached at the back to act like paddles. These flaps are light and buoyant and rotate from nine o'clock to 12 o'clock. The designer claims this makes them far superior to other inventions, which feature a six o'clock to nine o'clock rotation and allows the water walker to travel with some speed across the water surface. If the product ever gets off the ground – Rosen admits that, at the moment, 'it doesn't fit into an existing paradigm for sports' – then anglers may be able to do away with boats and walk straight out to where the piscatorial prey might be lying. Mr Rosen tested most of his prototypes on the Charles River; just what the fish made of it is anybody's guess.

A FEW FISHY FILMS TO SEE

A Plaice in the Sun
Down and Trout in Beverley Hills
The World According to Carp
Love is a Blenny Splendid Thing
Silence of the Clams

SEA TROUT PIONEERS

Hamish Stewart

The early half of the twentieth century saw a sudden burst of literature relating to the previously much ignored sea trout. Leading the way was Scottish angler Hamish Stewart with his *The Book of the Sea Trout* published in 1917. Stewart pushed back the barriers on how to fish for sea trout, declaring that the fish should be sought after in brackish water estuaries as well as up river and that they responded well to traditional brown trout flies. Prior to Stewart's observations, few bothered to fish exclusively for sea trout and those who did just whacked on a large salmon fly and left it at that, or simply caught sea trout by accident when salmon fishing. To these anglers, Stewart's book was a revelation.

NET THE CATCH

Fishermen worldwide use a variety of different nets to land their catch. These include:

Bag nets • Gill nets • Haaf nets
Herry-water nets • Ladle nets
Landing nets • Net and cobble
Poke nets • Seine nets • Shoulder nets
Stake nets • Stoop nets • Triangle nets
Whammel nets • Yair nets

A FISHY DELIGHT

The trout of the UK consume a varied diet of tasty morsels.
These are just a few items regularly on the trout's menu:

Snails
Freshwater shrimps
Beetles
Worms
Crayfish
Water louse
Limpets
Stonefly
Midges
Caddis fly
Mayfly
Sticklebacks
Small perch fry
Salmon eggs
Frogs and toads
Daddy long legs
Roach fry
Newts
Alder fly

FAMOUS LADIES IN FISHING

Miss Ballantine

In September 1922 Georgina Ballantine hooked a huge
salmon of 64lb on the Glendelvine beat of the River Tay.
Two hours later she landed it, albeit with a fair bit of
advice and encouragement from her father, an experienced
gillie, who was in the boat with her. To his credit he did not
once take over the rod from his daughter and with this
momentous catch she propelled herself forever into salmon
fishing history.

USELESS TACKLE

1. A waterproof jacket that leaks after only a micro split
2. Nylon stored in bright sunlight
3. Collapsible landing nets in need of Viagra
4. A reel full of grit
5. Hats that blow off
6. Breathable waders designed to take osmosis seriously

MAKING WADERS

The first waders to be used by anglers were little more than leather boots of various lengths, which, according to the old masters, afflicted the angler with cold feet, sciatica and rheumatism. However, with the invention of rubberised materials in the nineteenth century, anglers found they could wade for longer without suffering as many ailments. The first rubber boot waders were very heavy and stiff as a board, so what was gained in waterproofing was sadly lost in general comfort. Things improved from the 1950s when manufacturers got to grips with combining nylon and softer rubberised cloth materials. Suddenly wearing waders became more of a pleasure and less of an endurance test. Waterproof, 'breathable' materials are now commonly used in wader manufacture and these are a boon on a hot day; however, they have a higher tendency to leak at the seams than the old clumpy rubber boots. Swings and roundabouts.

FAMOUS ANGLERS AND THEIR DAY JOBS

Jeremy Paxman – Newsnight *presenter*
Chris Tarrant – *Television presenter*
Paul Young – *Scottish actor*

FISHING AND THE
ENVIRONMENT AGENCY

Most anglers know of the Environment Agency (EA)
because in England and Wales, they must pay their rod
licence fees direct to this government-led organisation.
However the EA is not just a licence fee collector, but
the principal body for the protection and enhancement
of the environment. It has no jurisdiction in Scotland
where a number of bodies exist to oversee different
aspects of the environment including, amongst others,
the Scottish Environmental Protection Agency (SEPA)
and Scottish National Heritage (SNH).

According to the its website, the Environment Agency
has the laudable aim of 'contributing to the sustainable
development and integrated management of air, land and
water thus ensuring a better quality of life for everyone,
now and for generations to come'. The Agency has
specific responsibilities regarding the management of
fisheries in terms of conservation, recreation, pollution
prevention and control, waste management, flood defence
and navigation of waterways. A wide-ranging not to say
challenging remit perhaps, but at least fish are rightfully
acknowledged as key indicators of the state of rivers and
lakes. After all, it is fish who are the first to go belly up
should a body of water become polluted in some way.
With this in mind one of the principal aims of the EA is
to help ensure healthy and abundant freshwater fish
stocks and populations. They do this by:

- Controlling the fishing pressure on waters through the
  issuing of the national rod licence and making relevant
  bylaws. These local fishery laws can cover anything
  from times of fishing to methods of angling.
- Ensuring the health and abundance of fish stocks by
  the regular surveying of fisheries.

- Preventing damage to fish and fish stocks by effective legal enforcement of fishery laws.
- Rescuing fish when pollution incidents occur and minimising damage to fish stocks.
- Carrying out habitat improvements for the benefit of resident fish.
- Constructing fish passes to allow migratory fish like salmon and sea trout free passage upriver to their spawning grounds.
- Monitoring the increase or decline in fish numbers in various waters by analysing anglers' catch returns, juvenile fish surveys and fish counters.
- Acting on the results of these surveys by advising on the stocking of fish to restore or improve a fishery.
- Carrying out fisheries research to assist future improvements and developments.

TERRIBLE FISHING JOKES

Q. What is the difference between a fish and a piano?
A. You can't tuna fish.

ANGLERS YOU MIGHT WANT TO AVOID

The Captain

Captains have seen military service or at least try hard to give that impression. They do everything in regimented fashion and hate any disruptions to routine like noisy children or small dogs. A typical fishing day will commence at 9.30am bang on, they stop for lunch exactly at 1pm and leave the water at 5pm precisely, fish activity or not. Captains are easily recognised by their back-slapping jollity, red faces and booming voices when their fishing has been productive. Equally they can be seen stamping around in furious temper blaming everyone else but themselves when they have failed to catch anything.

FISH WE SHOULD AVOID EATING

According to the Marine Conservation Society the list of fish below are taken from unsustainable fisheries, which are already severely overfished. In the interests of long-term conservation, the fish we should avoid eating include:

- American plaice
- Atlantic cod (from overfished stocks)
- Atlantic halibut
- Atlantic salmon (wild)
- Chilean sea bass
- Grey mullet
- Grouper
- Ling
- Marlin (blue, Indo Pacific and white)
- Patagonian Toothfish (sea bass)
- Rays
- Shark
- Skates
- Snapper
- Sturgeon
- Swordfish
- Turbot (from the North Sea)

SUPERSTITIONS OF THE SEAFARERS

Unlucky salmon

Salmon were considered by many seafarers to be an unlucky fish. Superstitious fishers in the North of Scotland would always refer to it as 'the red fish' rather than its true name. If a salmon was found on board a boat, this spelled disaster and its discovery would prevent the fishermen from setting sail that day. The reason behind this fear of salmon is unknown. It is doubly strange considering the symbolic links that Scottish salmon once had with various cities and the fact that they often appear in coats of arms.

SAVING THE GWYNIAD

As you have probably realised, the gwyniad is a fish of Welsh origin and a very rare one at that. To date, there is only one lake in North Wales left with a population of this unique herring-like species. The poor gwyniad has, in the past, been fished down almost to the point of extinction by netsmen eager to sell them as food. Now scientists are trying to reverse the decline and have set about conserving the remaining fish by trying to establish a separate population in a nearby lake. Rather than physically moving the endangered adult fish, they have been planting out fertilised eggs into the new water in the hope that some fish will grow on and establish new shoals of gwyniad.

REDS UNDER BEDS

Fish caught by anglers that have an association with the colour red:

Red drum – Also known as redfish or channel bass, this fish is found off the USA coast from Massachusetts to Mexico. They make delicious eating and are highly prized by anglers who consider them great sport.

Red fish – The red fish was an ancient name given to salmon by superstitious sea fisherman who considered them unlucky.

Red herrings – So called because the pungent preserving process rendered them red.

Red bellies – In the nineteenth century char were often referred to as red bellies owing to their reddish hue.

Red troots – In the eighteenth century Scottish brown trout were often known as 'red troots', perhaps because of their red flesh which made them good eating. How they made the transition from red to brown is lost in antiquity.

She's blown on that bloody porridge again

FOODY FLIES

Crab

Not only do oceanic fish such as bonefish and redfish consume other, smaller fish, but also they like eating crustaceans such as shrimp and small crabs. Designed by American fly fishers who fish predominantly in salt water, these 'flies' – and the term must be used loosely – look remarkably similar to little crawling crustaceans. Patterns known as 'flexo crabs' come complete with beady black eyes, skinny legs and mini pincers, all cleverly fashioned from fur and feather and slipped on to a small hook. Strictly for the specialist, these flies are so cute that they invariably attract plenty of jokes about well-dressed crab.

KINGS AND COMMONERS

This is the story of two fish, both the same species but very different bedfellows. On the one hand there is the King of Fish, the wild salmon, a silver, sleek, well muscled creature genetically imprinted to navigate thousands of miles to feed off the coast of Greenland before returning to its British river home. Not only that but the Atlantic salmon has the capacity to remember exactly which river it was born in and will only migrate to and from its own unique stream to spawn.

Compare this with what is now known as 'fake' salmon. These are farmed fish, lardy beasts bearing little resemblance to the real thing. They are grown from birth in a tank and forced to swim round and round forever in tightly packed circles. They are fed on pellets stained with a special dye to make their flesh seem pink (it's white-grey because they never get to eat what wild salmon do).

This is a salmon with all its journeyman genes missing. Because it's bred in a cage, the homing urge isn't there.

But does this matter? Farmed fish are apparently still fairly nutritious and cheap even if they are a bit clueless. However, they now pose a huge threat to our dwindling stock of wild fish. Their poorly-sited sea cages frequently break open in Atlantic storms and the fish with the non-existent long-term memory escape to sea, where they mix and mingle with wild ones.

Some farmed fish may even try and mate with native female salmon. If the daft ones spawn with the wild ones, ancient genetic lines will be severed and the subsequent offspring will be 'mongrel' hybrids, incapable of doing what wild salmon have been doing for centuries. Which could mean a catastrophic end for an already much exploited fish.

FISHES YOU MAY NOT HAVE HEARD OF

1. Bitterling – This is a small pretty-coloured fish with a deep blue-green sheen running along a flank of pink to light purple hue. It was first introduced to Britain in the 1920s, probably from eastern Asia to stock ornamental fish ponds. Bitterling are found in only a few select waters in Britain, mainly in the Midlands. Despite their scarcity they have a hardy constitution and are able to survive in murky waters, where most other species would go belly up.

2. Sunbleak – Another small rather cute looking fish with silvery flanks, green back and a blue sheen along its sides, the sunbleak is found at only a few sites in south west England. Sunbleak are not native to Britain and were first introduced in 1986 in the Hampshire area as ornamental fish. Because they are bossy little creatures which breed abundantly they are not welcome in UK waters where native fish populations exist.

3. Pumkinseed – A peculiar looking small fish rather like a mean looking goldfish with spiky fins and dusky bars along a deep flank of bronze laced with irregular blue green lines. The pumkinseed is an alien species introduced from America in the early 1900s. The fish prefer still waters and their presence is said to be spreading in waters in southern England where they are now considered a pest.

NICKNAMES FOR FISH

Coley – saithe
Cuddies – saithe
Finnock – young immature sea trout
Jack barrel – minnow
Kipper – dark red coloured salmon ready to spawn
Tiddlebat – three-spined stickleback

COCKNEY CASTING

In fly fishing, different situations on the river
call for different methods of casting, here are a
few Cockney versions:

Tray Cast – Spey cast
Twitch Cast – Switch cast
Upnose Cast – Overhead cast
Stroll Cast – Roll cast
Beetle Cast – Steeple cast
Bubble Call – Double haul

FISH WARS

Icy stares across the Med

In mid-June 2003, a Spanish armed patrol boat intercepted a Moroccan fishing vessel 37 miles off the coast of Lanzarote. Its crew comprised of 15 Moroccans and four Spanish chancers, and its hold contained 4,500 kilos of fish and prawns. The crew told the unconvinced Spanish authorities that the catch was obtained in Moroccan waters. This incident was merely an addition to a long-running territorial dispute between Spain and Morocco, dating right back to Morocco's former status as a French and Spanish protectorate. Fishing disputes between the two countries have been traditionally bilateral, but more recently have been co-ordinated by the EU. As the only oil-free North African country, Morocco depends upon high seas fishing for economic survival, but the Spanish argue that this has led it to dip into their waters far too often. To complicate matters, the countries have also tussled over a one kilometre-wide islet, Perejil, in the Straits of Gibraltar. It is, of course, totally uninhabited.

A BIT FISHY

Which warm-blooded mammal shares its name with
both a type of fish and a type of fly?
Answer on page 144.

JUST AN ILLUSION

In the good old days, coarse fishing used to be about catching perhaps a dace or a gudgeon (both not much bigger than a few ounces) on a tiny hook while sitting quietly at the side of a river or canal. It was a simple, basic skill and you felt mighty proud of what you had achieved. However since the 1980s, coarse fishing has undergone a revolution. The popularity of stocked commercial 'fisheries' – anything from an artificial concrete bowl of a pond to a flooded gravel pit – took off in a big way over 20 years ago and has never looked back. Anglers brought up on these fisheries, which are in the main stocked with big carp, largely mock the old ways. Why struggle to get to a quiet spot on the riverbank, search out swims and modify tackle when all you need to do with the new ponds is drive straight to the lakeside, switch on your i-Pod and hey presto within five minutes you hook an enormous fish about the size of a small child. Heavy stocking almost ensures that you will catch a monster, and quickly too.

Many dedicated fishermen and women are beginning to think twice about this new fishery ethos. Fishing, they say, used to require a bit of skill and water craft, but nowadays there doesn't seem to be quite the same challenge involved. They are worried that newcomers to the sport will think that if that's all there is to it, why bother? And they would have a point...

SCOTLAND'S ALL-BUT-FORGOTTEN TWENTIETH CENTURY FISHING HEROES

RC Bridgett

During the latter half of the nineteenth century it became fashionable among the angling intelligentsia to deride the sport of trout loch fishing as greatly inferior when compared to the same sport done on a river. Basically, their reasoning boiled down to some ill-informed thinking mixed with a fair bit of 'lowland' versus 'highland' snobbery. Bridgett saw this with astute clarity and did much to reverse the trend. He wrote most of his books in the 1920s, of which *Loch Fishing in Theory and Practice* was the most erudite and the most successful. Bridgett is most famous for dispelling what he called 'a charge against the loch'. Though few modern anglers remember him now, Bridgett's lucid writings have gone a long way towards helping loch anglers to go about their business without feeling little better than lepers.

FOODY FLIES

Olives

Banish any image of a trout rising to a cocktail stick impaled with a piquant Greek olive, perhaps spiked with a red dash of pimento. What fishermen are talking about here is an insect known as an 'olive'. These are upwinged flies related to the mayfly and when they hatch on a river or lake, trout feed on them avidly. Probably because olives are such a prolific British insect, some of the earliest flies ever made, which was somewhere around the fourteenth century, vaguely resembled olives with their prominent wing and dark body. Olives that the trout find tasty include the 'lake olive', 'medium olive', 'large dark olive', 'pond olive', 'rough olive' and 'blue winged olive'.

TERRIBLE FISHING JOKES

'I was fishing off the pier when, would you believe it, a little sand eel no bigger than my pinkie took the bait. Next a big cod came along and swallowed the sand eel but before I could get the cod reeled in a shark appeared and grabbed the cod.'

'Did you land the shark?'

'No, the bloody eel let go.'

I NAME THIS TROUT

The trout of the Northern Hemisphere all come under the genus *Salmo trutta* yet have a huge range of names. Here are but a few;

Black finned trout • Brook trout • Brownies
Bull trout • Ferox • Finnock • Gillaroo
Golden trout • Sewin • Slob trout
Sonaghen • White trout

'WE SHALL FIGHT THEM ON THE BEACHES'

It is said that Winston Churchill got the idea for what became one of his most rousing speeches in 1938 while cod fishing on a beach at Dungeness. Churchill was not only a keen sea angler, but also gained much inspiration from the simple pleasures of coarse fishing. The smoking room at Blenheim Palace once carried photographs of Churchill and Field Marshall Montgomery doing battle, not with the dogs of war, but with small rudd on English rivers like the Avon or Kennet. Here they would stretch out their roach poles, don their old leather bait aprons, launch a fine mix of ground bait, catch innumerable small fishes, chew on fine cigars and almost certainly muse on world events.

YOU WEIR IT WELL

In Wales one of the earliest forms of fishing was not with rod and line, but by making a 'weir'. A small wall or dam would be made either from stones or wooden sticks and this would be placed across the river once a good head of migratory fish like salmon and trout had run upstream. The weir effectively trapped the fish in the shallows. It would then simply be a case of every man for himself, as the hapless fish were jumped on and speared either with a crude harpoon or a three-pronged trident. In Scotland, similar early methods of fish catching are known as 'cruives', whereas in England the ancient fishermen simply referred to them as 'fish dams' or 'traps'.

TOO MUCH OF A GOOD THING

While fish like a bit of shade to give them cover from predators, too much of a good thing has the opposite effect and our finny friends do not flourish. In 2005, the River Yealm in Devon had got so overgrown with non native laurel bushes that the Environment Agency decided to put their laudable Salmon Action Plan into operation. This involved a team armed with axe and buzz saw removing several tonnes of dense leafy cover and thinning out the canopy sufficiently for light to penetrate the dark pools again. This was intended to increase the biodiversity of all aquatic species and, it is hoped, to raise salmon survival rates by giving them back their natural range of food sources.

FISHY FIGURES

30

Length, in yards, of a standard Cortland fly line

ANGLERS YOU WON'T MIND
MEETING ON THE RIVERBANK

The Oracle

The font of all angling wisdom, this fisher is often the most unassuming and ordinary guy on the bank. As they are becoming increasingly rare, you should cherish their company. You will know when you come across an Oracle, as half your day will be gone in deep conversation yet you never think begrudgingly of this lost time. Oracles exhibit a fair degree of eccentricity. They are incapable of remembering the time and cannot for the life of them operate a mobile phone; however, there is a sagely confidence to their fishing, which leaves most of us for dead.

LETS GET FINNY

Despite being apparently small appendages, fins are terribly important to the survival of a fish. Quite simply, few fish species can do without them, for they are needed to propel the fish along, help the fish keep their balance in a current and either speed up or slow. Two pectoral fins help to stabilise the fish and to change the direction in which it swims. The two pelvic fins and the one anal fin help the fish to rise and fall in the water while the dorsal and caudal (tail) fin act both as rudders and as the main means of propulsion. Though the classifications are seldom used now, fish can be divided into groups by the nature of their fins. 'Acanthopterygians' from the Greek akantha meaning thorn and 'pterugion' meaning wing are fish with spiny rays such as bass, perch or zander. 'Malacopterygians' from the Greek word malakos meaning soft are soft finned fishes like herring, trout or pike.

*What do you mean, you dropped
my Hardy rod over the side?*

ANGLING PLOYS
THAT DIDN'T CATCH ON

Hollow butts

In the mid nineteenth century rods with hollow butt
sections were made in Scotland. The idea of these was to
store spare rod tips. The fine tips of the old fly rods were
notoriously brittle and often broke while fishing. Rather
than have to give up his sport, the angler could simply take
out a replacement and attach it then and there.
Unfortunately the hollow butt made the rod extremely
difficult to cast with and the idea had to be dropped,
although it was not entirely buried, as telescopic rods came
into production in the 1960s.

ALL THE BETTER TO SEE YOU WITH

Swordfish, tuna and marlin native to the Pacific Ocean have been found to be capable of improving their vision using what can only be described as centrally-heated eyeballs. Apparently they have a specially adapted heating organ in the muscle adjacent to their large ball shaped eyes. This has the effect of warming their eyes, which in turn greatly enhances their ability to spot prey at greater distances. It seems that evolution of the species has produced specially tailored retinas, which when heated allow the swordfish to capture the available light more quickly and see better. This phenomenon is even odder when you consider the rest of the fish's body remains cold-blooded. Although the fish see their prey better, heated eyeballs do not help them to distinguish between real food and anglers' artificial lures.

BEASTLY POACHING

Poaching of freshwater fish has been around ever since man discovered he could make money from selling the catch without paying to fish for it. For centuries the salmon has fallen foul of poaching. Here are a few examples of particularly nasty methods:

1. Leistering
2. Ottering
3. Netting
4. Sniggling
5. Worming
6. Prawning
7. Dragging
8. Burning
9. Cyaniding
10. Dynamiting

GAME TACKLE

Sometimes you will meet a fly fisher by the river, who appears to be weighed down with fishing accoutrements dangling about his person. These are likely to include:

A zillion boxes of flies for every occasion
Spare spools
A landing net
Nylon with droppers
Nylon without droppers
Zingers
Gink bottles (makes flies float)
Zink bottles (makes them sink)
Line tray
Fluorocarbon
Nippers
Fly patches

SOMETHING IN THE WATER

Male fish species are coming under increasing threat from the amounts of hormone-altering substances being found in groundwater and watercourses throughout the UK. While it might be thought that this is putting fish in touch with their feminine side, in the long term there could be such a major reduction of productivity in various fish species, and fragile fish populations could become extinct. It seems the fish are absorbing endocrine disruptors, which come from, among other sources, pesticides, plasticisers, PCBs and synthetic and natural oestrogens. As a consequence of this insidious and ever-present pollution, male fish are becoming feminised.

The male gudgeon, for example, has been particularly hard hit, with eggs appearing in the testes. It has not taken to cross-dressing as yet.

Women! Never here when you need 'em

HOW FISH GOT THEIR NAMES

Grayling

Ancient anglers who caught grayling noticed the fish have a light smell of the herb thyme about them, hence their Latin name *Thymallus*. Up until the late eighteenth century, the grayling was also known as the 'umber', meaning shadow, presumably a name derived from its dark secretive outline. 'The Lady of the Stream' is another handle for grayling first coined in the nineteenth century by esteemed English angler Francis Francis who said: 'If the trout be the gentleman of the streams, the grayling is certainly the lady.' The fish are relatively common across most of England, parts of Wales and as far north in Scotland as Perthshire.

RECYCLING YOUR FISHING LURES

Americans love their beer and their fishing, often, but not necessarily always, in that order. Now a company called www.bottlecaplure.com have come up with the ingenious idea of using all those spent bottle caps to catch fish. The company recycles the caps, flattens them out, reshapes them and then attaches a treble hook to fashion them into a spinning lure. Apparently the bottle cap lure has been very successful in catching a variety of fish species including walleye, salmon, trout, bass, char and perch.

A BIT FISHY

Which fish was called the nurse fish because of its supposed medicinal powers?
Answer on page 144.

GERR 'ORFE

Though orfe are eaten in both Russia and Finland where they are reared as farmed fish, the Brits are none too keen on them as a foodstuff, and instead either fish for them or keep them as pets in little ponds. The orfe (also known as the ide) is a spanking little fish reminiscent of a silvery goldfish, but larger. It comes in other colours notably blue or gold. These are non-native fish and were first introduced to Britain from Germany in the latter half of the nineteenth century. The fish were taken first to stock the lakes and ponds of Woburn Abbey, but further introductions have seen orfe spread across the UK, for both ornamental and sporting use. Coarse anglers generally rate them highly and the popularity of orfe fishing is on the up in the UK.

TAKE ONE SWIM FEEDER

The main role of the coarse fisher's swim feeder is to liven up the fish in front of him. This it does by being cast out full of bait, such as maggots or special mixes, which then slowly disperses through the current, attracting fish to feed from far and wide, which the angler then tries to catch with rod and line. Like so much in fishing tackle today, there is a considerable variety of these secret weapons, including:

Block end feeders
Early method feeders
Fatal Attractors
Fox feeders
Maggot feeders
Method feeders
Oblong feeders
Open-ended feeders
Round feeders
Spods

HAIR WINGS

It is thought that the originator of flies made with hair, as opposed to filaments from feather wings, was a rancher from Idaho. Apparently in the 1890s he took to dressing his fishing flies with tufts of bucktail. While the rest of Europe was intent on making ever more delicate flies of fur and exotic feather, the Americans would have no such pretensions and persisted with incorporating hair into the fly body and wings. Apart from bucktail, their fly tyers also took to using bear, squirrel, coyote, deer and wood chuck hair. This across-the-pond split in fly tying skills persisted until about the 1980s, when the Brits finally absorbed some of the American novelties into their fly boxes.

A FEW FISHY FILMS TO SEE

The Cod Father
Bream Streets
Jack the Kipper
Some Pike it Hot

FAMOUS ANGLERS WHO NEVER WERE

J R Hartley

A popular *Yellow Pages* advert featured an actor playing the part of an elderly gentleman who, having tried a few places in the directory, finally found a bookshop which stocked a tome that he had written, entitled *Fly Fishing* by J R Hartley.

Mr Crabtree

Beginning in 1947 the *Daily Mirror* carried a very successful cartoon-style column called *Mr Crabtree goes Fishing*. In it a wise elderly gent advises his young protégé Peter on the finer arts of fishing. Mr Crabtree did not exist, however, and was created by esteemed English angler Bernard Venables, who died in his ninety-fourth year in 2001.

Brad Pitt

In the film directed by Robert Redford *A River Runs through It*, the character played by Brad Pitt appears to be an expert caster and catcher of fish. In fact, most if not all his fly fishing sequences were ghosted by expert US anglers, including the great Jason Borger, who executed the famous 'shadow casting' sequence.

TERRIBLE FISHING JOKES

Q: What is the best way to talk to a fish?
A: Drop it a line.

A BIT FISHY

The answers. As if you needed them.

P6. Redbelly tilapia, an Egyptian fish introduced to the UK, which has bred in the wild in Wales.

P13. They are all types of Irish char.

P20. Trout. The colours all describe European trout except for the blue trout, which is a hybrid, a European trout cross-bred with an American rainbow trout.

P25. They are used as bait to catch a bigger fish.

P28. In a lake. This is the Latin name for a North American lake trout.

P42. Whiting, herring, sparling, houting, whitling and ling (you could also have bitterling if you are really clever).

P48. Grouse. Its feathers are still used to construct certain types of fishing flies; the other birds' feathers are no longer used, as the birds are protected species.

P75. These are different types of nymphs, which form a staple part of the diet of a trout.

P92. In fly fishing this was the forerunner of what is now known as 'false casting'. In the nineteenth century a fly could be dried in the air by a swishing cast known as the carshalton dodge.

P98. The odd one out is houting, which is a white fish; all the others are obscure names for the allis shad.

P105. Nineteenth-century salmon poachers based on the River Wye, southern England.

P113. The odd one out is thorm, which is made up; all the others are old colloquial names for the sea trout.

P132. The wolf. There is a wolf fish and an American fly known as 'the grey wulff'.

P141. The tench.

FURTHER READING

Where to Fly Fish in Britain and Ireland, J Bailey

The Bright Stream of Memory, G Bucknall

Trout Fishers Handbook, L Crawford

Freshwater Fishing, Falkus and Buller

The Fly, A Herd,

Fishing and Thinking, AA Luce

A Dictionary of Fly Fishing, CB McCully

Where the Bright Waters Meet, Plunket Greene

Early Scottish Angling Literature, Professor NW Simmonds

The Wildlife Series – Trout, Edited by Stolz and Schnell

NOTES, THOUGHTS AND JOTTINGS

NOTES, THOUGHTS AND JOTTINGS

NOTES, THOUGHTS AND JOTTINGS

NOTES, THOUGHTS AND JOTTINGS

NOTES, THOUGHTS AND JOTTINGS

NOTES, THOUGHTS AND JOTTINGS

NOTES, THOUGHTS AND JOTTINGS

NOTES, THOUGHTS AND JOTTINGS

NOTES, THOUGHTS AND JOTTINGS

NOTES, THOUGHTS AND JOTTINGS

NOTES, THOUGHTS AND JOTTINGS

NOTES, THOUGHTS AND JOTTINGS

NOTES, THOUGHTS AND JOTTINGS

NOTES, THOUGHTS AND JOTTINGS

WE HAD A WHALE OF A TIME

Thanks to the following who gillied so well:
Margaret Buxton; Ewan, Andrew, Ron, Bea and Betty
'Spike' Crawford; Hazel Mendonca; Howard Montague;
and all the thinkers at Think Publishing.